REVELATION
AND THE
GENERAL
EPISTLES

THE SERIES

INTERPRETER'S CONCISE COMMENTARY

REVELATION
AND THE
GENERAL
EPISTLES
A COMMENTARY ON
HEBREWS, JAMES, I & II PETER,
I, II, & III JOHN, JUDE, REVELATION

By
Warren A. Quanbeck,
Richard L. Scheef, Jr.,
Claude Holmes Thompson,
Massey H. Shepherd, Jr.,
and S. MacLean Gilmour

Edited by Charles M. Laymon

Abingdon Press
Nashville

Interpreter's Concise Commentary
Volume VIII: REVELATION AND THE GENERAL EPISTLES

Library of Congress Cataloging in Publication Data

Main entry under title:
Revelation and the General Epistles.
    (Interpreter's concise commentary; v. 8)
    "Previously published . . . as part of *The Interpreter's one-volume
commentary on the bible*"—Verso t.p.
    Bibliography: p.
    1. Bible. N.T. Hebrews—Commentaries. 2. Bible. N.T. Catholic
Epistles—Commentaries. 3. Bible. N.T. Revelation—Commen-
taries. I. Quanbeck, Warren A. II. Laymon, Charles M.
III. Series.
BS2775.3.R48   1983   227'.907   83-7089

ISBN 0-687-19239-0

(Previously published by Abingdon Press in cloth as part of
The Interpreter's One-Volume Commentary on the Bible, regular ed.
ISBN 0-687-19299-4, thumb-indexed ed. ISBN 0-687-19300-1.)

MANUFACTURED BY THE PARTHENON PRESS AT
NASHVILLE, TENNESSEE, UNITED STATES OF AMERICA

EDITOR'S PREFACE

to the original edition

A significant commentary on the Bible is both timely and timeless. It is timely in that it takes into consideration newly discovered data from many sources that are pertinent in interpreting the Scriptures, new approaches and perspectives in discerning the meaning of biblical passages, and new insights into the relevancy of the Bible for the times in which we live. It is timeless since it deals with the eternal truths of God's revelation, truths of yesterday, today, and of all the tomorrows that shall be.

This commentary has been written within this perspective. Its authors were selected because of their scholarship, their religious insight, and their ability to communicate with others. Technical discussions do not protrude, yet the most valid and sensitive use of contemporary knowledge underlies the interpretations of the several writings. It has been written for ministers, lay and nonprofessional persons engaged in studying or teaching in the church school, college students and those who are unequipped to follow the more specialized discussions of biblical matters, but who desire a thoroughly valid and perceptive guide in interpreting the Bible.

The authorship of this volume is varied in that scholars were chosen from many groups to contribute to the task. In this sense it is an ecumenical writing. Protestants from numerous denominations, Jews, and also Roman Catholics are represented in the book. Truth cannot be categorized according to its ecclesiastical sources. It is above and beyond such distinctions.

It will be noted that the books of the Apocrypha have been included and interpreted in the same manner as the canonical writings. The value of a knowledge of this body of literature for understanding the historical background and character of the Judaic-Christian tradition has been widely recognized in our time, but commentary treatments of it have not been readily accessible. In addition, the existence of the Revised Standard Version and the New English Bible translations of these documents makes such a commentary upon them as is included here both necessary and significant.

The commentary as a whole avoids taking dogmatic positions or representing any one particular point of view. Its authors were chosen throughout the English-speaking field of informed and recognized biblical scholars. Each author was urged to present freely his own interpretation and, on questions where there was sometimes a diversity of conclusions, each was also asked to define objectively the viewpoints of others while he was offering and defending his own.

Many persons have contributed to the writing and production of this volume. One of the most rewarding of my personal experiences as editor was corresponding with the authors. On every hand there was enthusiasm for the project and warmth of spirit. The authors' commitment to the task and their scholarly sensitivity were evident in all of my relationships with them. The considerate judgments of the manuscript consultants, Morton S. Enslin, Dwight M. Beck, W. F. Stinespring, Virgil M. Rogers, and William L. Reed, were invaluable in the making of the character of the commentary. The copy editors who have worked under the careful and responsible guidance of Mr. Gordon Duncan of Abingdon Press have contributed greatly to the accuracy and readability of the commentary.

—Charles M. Laymon, Editor

PUBLISHER'S PREFACE

The intent of the *Interpreter's Concise Commentary* is to make available to a wider audience the commentary section of *The Interpreter's One-Volume Commentary on the Bible*. In order to do this, the Publisher is presenting the commentary section of the original hardback in this eight-volume paperback set. At the same time, and in conjunction with our wish to make *The Interpreter's One-Volume Commentary* more useful, we have edited the hardback text for the general reader: we have defined most of the technical terms used in the original hardback text; we have tried to divide some of the longer sentences and paragraphs into shorter ones; we have tried to make the sexually stereotyped language used in the original commentary inclusive where it referred to God or to both sexes; and we have explained abbreviations, all in an attempt to make the text more easily read.

The intention behind this paperback arrangement is to provide a handy and compact commentary on those individual sections of the Bible that are of interest to readers. In this paperback format we have not altered the substance of any of the text of the original hardback, which is still available. Rather, our intention is to smooth out some of the scholarly language in order to make the text easier to read. We hope this arrangement will make this widely accepted commentary on the Bible even more profitable for all students of God's Word.

WRITERS

Warren A. Quanbeck
Professor of Systematic Theology, Luther Theological Seminary, St. Paul, Minnesota

Richard L. Scheef, Jr.
Professor of New Testament, Eden Theological Seminary, Webster Groves, Missouri

Claude Holmes Thompson
Professor of Systematic Theology, Candler School of Theology, Emory University, Atlanta, Georgia

Massey H. Shepherd, Jr.
Hodges Professor of Liturgics, The Church Divinity School of the Pacific, Berkeley, California

S. MacLean Gilmour
Late Norris Professor of New Testament, Andover Newton Theological Seminary, Newton Centre, Massachusetts

CONTENTS

THE LETTER TO THE HEBREWS

Warren A. Quanbeck

INTRODUCTION

Authorship

A very old tradition, preserved in the Vulgate and in the King
James Version, ascribes Hebrews to Paul. But when we examine
the book itself, and ancient references to it, we discover that its
authorship is uncertain. Also we know very little about its
origin, destination, and date. It is difficult to determine even
why the letter was written, and modern interpreters differ on
this question.

The earliest known quotation from the book appears in a letter
of Clement of Rome usually dated around A.D. 96. From this and
other citations we learn that it was known very early in the
western part of the church. However, it was not ascribed to Paul
until the fourth century. The story is different in the east. Here
it was ascribed to Paul as early as the second century. Yet
scholars in Alexandria, especially Origen, had their doubts
about Pauline authorship because it differed from the Pauline
letters in literary style and theological language.

Detailed study in modern times has led to almost unanimous
agreement that the language, style, and ideas differ markedly
from those of Paul. It is almost inconceivable that he could have
been the author. Origen long ago observed that God alone really

1

knows who the author was. Modern scholarship has been unable to improve on this verdict.

The book itself tells us a good deal about the kind of person the author was. He had an excellent command of Greek. He wrote with a refined and elegant style which no translation conveys adequately. He read his Old Testament in Greek, for he always quotes the Septuagint, the Bible of Greek-speaking Jews and Christians. His world of thought was dominated by the tradition of worship, and he saw Jesus Christ as the fulfillment of the sacrificial system.

He also knew the speculations of the Alexandrian Jewish philosopher Philo. But unlike Philo he did not fit biblical ideas into the Hellenistic thought world. He took his material from thinkers like Philo, but he fitted them into a biblical framework. There is a distinction between the shadow world of matter and the real world of spirit, which he set in the framework of the history of salvation. He therefore refused to discount the created world of time and space. Instead of the allegorical interpretation of the Old Testament favored by Philo and others he preferred the typological. That is, he found in the ancient stories "types" or analogies of truths fully revealed in Christ.

Though he was a subtle, profound, and at times abstruse theologian, the author shows himself as practical. The preacher in him takes over frequently. There are passages of exhortation which seek to apply the truth of theology to the situation of his readers. His combination of literary skill and pastoral concern has produced some of the most eloquent and moving passages in the New Testament. People who have no detailed acquaintance with the book still know such expressions as "since we are surrounded by so great a cloud of witnesses" (12:1), "Jesus Christ is the same yesterday and today and for ever" (13:8), "we have no lasting city" (13:14), and the glowing benediction of 13:20-21.

Origin and Destination
While the book tells us something about its author, it gives us almost no information about where it was written and to whom it

was addressed. The closing greeting mentions "those who come from Italy" (13:24). This has usually been interpreted as a message sent home by Italians who were with the author. Thus it is said to be evidence that the book is a letter written from a place outside Italy and addressed to a group inside Italy, probably at Rome. The fact that the first known citation of the work is by Clement of Rome lends some support to this theory. On the other hand the Greek phrase translated "those who come from Italy" is ambiguous (see below on 13:24). It may mean simply "Italians"—that is, native members of a church in Italy as distinguished from visiting missionaries.

Furthermore it is not certain that this greeting was an original part of the work. The book has traditionally been called a letter on the basis of the final paragraph (13:22-25) and the personal request for intercessory prayer (13:18-19). But actually this work has more the literary character of a treatise or a homily, a sermonic exhortation. For this reason some have suggested that an editor, noting the popularity of Paul's letters, composed an epistolary ending after the Pauline pattern (cf. II Corinthians 1:11-12 and Philippians 2:19, 23-24; 4:20-22). He added it in the hope of attracting more readers by giving the impression of a letter.

In fact there has been much discussion on whether all of chapter 13 may be an addition. Obviously it does not fit into the close-knit structure of chapters 1–12. If a second author produced it, however, he was clearly one who shared the same world of ideas, and was trained in the same school of rhetoric, for both thought and style are similar to those of the original author. It seems more probable, therefore, that chapter 13—or at least verses 1-17—was composed by the same author as chapters 1–12. It was either an original part of the work for the purpose of including some practical afterthoughts, or possibly as a later supplement to commend it to a new group of readers. It may even have been a separate writing which was joined to the longer work by an editor. Nevertheless assuming that all of chapter 13 was an original part of the work gives us little help in

3

identifying either the place of writing or the readers to whom it was addressed.

If the book was intended as a letter, it perhaps originally had an epistolary introduction. This might have been lost in transmission or perhaps was dropped by an editor seeking to circulate it beyond the group addressed. If so, it is barely possible that the title "to the Hebrews" had some basis in the text. Otherwise the title must be viewed as an editorial interpretation of the content and thus gives little clue to the original address.

In any case the phrase is not very specific. It could mean either Jews or Jewish Christians. The latter designation might apply to many different communities in the early church. Some scholars in recent times have defended the title "to the Hebrews" in the sense of Jewish Christians. But most have challenged it, and have shown how little support the text provides. They see the arguments of the book as aimed at Gentile Christians, or at Christians in general. These were well acquainted with the Septuagint, which was the Bible of the early church, but knew little or nothing of contemporary Judaism.

Date

Nor can the date be fixed with precision. The citation of the work by Clement of Rome about A.D. 96 indicates that it was in circulation by that time. The lack of any reference to the destruction of the Jerusalem temple has been urged as evidence that it originated before 70. But since the author is interested in the tabernacle rather than the temple, this argument from silence is of doubtful significance. In fact it has been suggested that the author avoids mentioning the temple because he was writing after it had been destroyed.

More significant are the exhortations in the text to endurance and discipline (see 3:14; 10:23, 36; 12:1-11; cf. chapter 11). These verses may imply that the readers face the threat of persecution. Also important is mention of "former days" (10:32-34) when the readers suffered a period of persecution. Earlier commentators interpreted these as evidence that the book was written during or shortly before the persecution of Roman Christians by Nero in 64-67. Assuming the readers to be Jewish Christians in Rome, they took the "former days" to be the period when Claudius banished the Jews from the city (Acts 18:2). Recent interpreters, however, have been more inclined to take the persecution of "former days" as that under Nero. They see the present threat as either a danger that faced a particular Christian group thereafter or a general persecution of Christians believed to have occurred in the reign of Domitian (81-96).

Significant also are the evidences that the readers are Christians of the second or third generation—for example, 2:3; 5:12 and 6:1. Some scholars have found what they claim to be signs that the author was acquainted with a number of Paul's letters. It appears that these letters were not generally circulated until after the publication of Acts. Thus such clues, if valid, would date the book in the last decade or so before its citation by Clement. If the reference to Timothy (see below on 13:23) is an original part of the book, however, it suggests that the author had some contact with the missionary circle gathered by Paul. No doubt many of the apostle's ideas and expressions long persisted in the preaching and teaching of this group. Thus there seems to be no firm basis for fixing a precise date. The book was evidently written sometime during the period between about 60 and 96.

Purpose

The traditional assumption, expressed in the title, is that the book was addressed to Jewish Christians. On this basis the author's purpose has commonly been described as strengthening the faith of readers about to abandon their commitment, perhaps under pressure of persecution, and return to the religion of the synagogue. Close study of the text, however, shows that it fails to deal with the real issues between the early church and the synagogue. Modern scholars who defend the traditional address, therefore, see a somewhat different purpose. One suggestion is that those addressed are members of a conservative, legalistic community. They interpret the gospel within the framework of Judaism rather than as fulfillment of the old covenant. The author's purpose then is to win them to an understanding of the gospel along the lines of Stephen or of Paul—a gospel which sees the dynamic and creative elements set in motion by Jesus Christ and grasps the missionary, expansionist character of Christianity.

A majority of modern interpreters believe the book is addressed to Christians whose "Hebrew" background is limited to the Septuagint. The author's purpose then may best be seen in his exhortations. These are aimed at readers whom he views as in danger, not of apostasy, but of inattention, complacency, and drifting into unbelief. He is seeking not so much to strengthen the commitment of new converts as to reawaken the lost zeal and fervor of longtime Christians. Thus in his writing he combines theological argument and homiletical exhortation. He seeks to both inform his readers and persuade them to perseverance, self-discipline, and mutual love. The understanding of the role of Christ which he presents is intended not merely for contemplation but for appropriation and action.

Distinctive Features

One of the most prominent elements in the book—and one of the most puzzling to the modern reader—is the use made of Old Testament quotations. One trained in contemporary literary and historical method may suspect the author of unhistorical, allegorical, and arbitrary interpretations and thus discount his argument. For the author and for his readers the Septuagint was the authoritative Bible. Problems concerning its accuracy did not occur to them. We use an English text translated from the Hebrew, and at times it does not seem to support the author's point.

In some cases (1:5-13; 5:5; 6:14) the author uses the Old Testament as though it were a direct quotation from God. Examination of these passages in their original setting shows that he has grasped the main thrust of most of them. The divergence from modern interpretation is not so great as one at first supposes. In two instances (2:12; 10:5-7) he uses the Old Testament as a quotation from the preexistent Christ. These are hardly persuasive to a modern reader. But it should be noted that the author's christological convictions do not rest solely on these passages. On the basis of many testimonies he has come to his faith that Jesus is Lord and Son of God. In these two passages he finds a confirmation which seems to him remarkable and to us accidental. His convictions, however, are not threatened if the witness of these passages is withheld.

Much has also been made of the presence of Platonic ideas in the book. The contrast of the earthly tabernacle as shadow with the heavenly sanctuary as reality is basic to the argument. The death of Christ is seen first of all as an event in the eternal world of God, the self-giving of God to creatures. But it is also an event in human history, the Crucifixion. This may be a derivative from the Platonic philosophy common in the first century. The ideas of Alexandrian Jews such as Philo have undoubtedly influenced the author. But their Platonic character is often overstated and their constant connection with the biblical history of salvation overlooked or underestimated.

The idea that Christ has offered the true and complete sacrifice and that he now ministers as priest in the real, the heavenly, sanctuary is certainly basic to the book. The interpretation of the fulfillment of the Old Testament, the old covenant, the sacrificial cultus, and even prophetic ethics all depend on it. But these ideas are set in the midst of a dynamic historical understanding of the unfolding purpose of God. Also permeating the book are ideas of eschatology—the anticipation that God will soon catastrophically bring the present age to an end and inaugurate a new age. Examples are the world to come (2:5), the urgency of today (3:7, 15), the present era as the last time (1:2; 3:14; 6:11), and the stress on the once-for-all character of Christ's offering (7:27; 9:12; 10:10).

Even the idea of perfection may be wrongly read as a Platonic term, overlooking its eschatological character as applied to Christ (cf. 2:10; 5:9; 7:28) and to the Christian (cf. 10:14; 11:40; 12:23). The eschatological ideas are indeed remarkably similar to contemporary developmental ideas in taking seriously the notions of time, movement, and growth.

I. THE THEME (1:1-4)

This opening statement (all of verses 1-4) is a single long, sonorous sentence in elegant Greek. It introduces the theme of the work and connects it with the religious traditions of the immediate past. In a few pregnant phrases it indicates the central significance of Jesus Christ in the working out of the purpose of God.

1:1. *God's Revelation to Humanity.* The author assumes that his readers share his attitude toward the religious traditions of Israel. God has spoken **to our fathers** at various times and in **various ways.** What the prophets spoke and wrote was the word of God—God's own address to creatures. This is not only information about God but a personal word spoken by God. In this word God is open to human beings, admits them to the divine presence, is bestowed on them in fellowship. The prophetic tradition knows it is the bearer of the wonderful gift of the knowledge of the God who made and sustains the world. God has established a covenant with Israel. God has granted them the knowledge of God's love for all beings, and called them to be the servants of mercy.

1:2-4. *Jesus as God's Ultimate Revelation.* In view of this lofty estimate of the traditions of Israel, what the author has to say about Jesus Christ is quite moving in its impact. He regards Christ the Son as bringing fulfillment of the purposes of God. He ascribes to him a series of titles and accomplishments. **These last days** refers to the time of fulfillment of the purpose of God spoken of in the Old Testament. The climax of God's working in history has appeared in the career of the man Jesus of Nazareth. His life and mission, his death and resurrection comprise God's final speech to humans. What God began to say through the prophets of Israel God has now brought to completion in this person.

God has condescended to use human language in order to

speak to creatures. What God has to say finally could not be expressed in words alone but took the form of a human life—a life whose obedience and dedication mark the turning point of human history and embody God's love. The decisive revelation of God is given, not in a document, but in a person. The rest of verses 1-4 describe who this person is.

1:2a. The meaning of **Son** here is that of the Old Testament tradition: one who has a unique relationship to the Father, one who carries out the will and purpose of the Father, and who therefore has a unique and supreme revelatory function. But though the author applies very exalted titles to the Son, he also maintains the distinction between Father and Son. He consistently subordinates the Son to the Father.

The titles and activities ascribed to the Son in the following verses, however, certainly strain this Old Testament language to its uttermost limits. They push strongly in the direction of the language of the Nicene Creed, in which the fourth century church declared the Son to be "very God of very God, . . . of one substance with the Father."

1:2b. Because he is the Son, he is also **heir of all things.** All human wisdom, wealth, and glory are properly his. All human suffering, defeat, and disgrace he also makes his own. It is the teaching of the gospels that the way to honor is the way of the cross.

1:2c. Late Jewish theology saw wisdom as the power of God and the agent of creation. In Hellenistic Christianity the Son was identified as the Logos, or Word, of God, **through whom . . . he created the world** (cf. John 1:3).

1:3a. The Greek word translated **reflects** may mean also "radiates." This would imply a more active role. "Reflects" suggests that "the Son can do . . . only what he sees the Father doing" (John 5:19). More important, the New Testament gives new meaning to the word **glory.** Secular conceptions of glory are equivalent to fame or good report, but this term acquires new meaning when it is seen in the light of the Son's obedience unto death. It is the special glory of God that God is given in the service of creation.

9

The image in **bears the very stamp of his nature** is of the impress of a seal in wax or clay. As the impression of the seal testifies to the origin of a letter so the mission of the Son shows its origin in the will of the Father. When one encounters the Son, one observes the sign of the Father's activity. **Upholding the universe** expresses the Old Testament idea of creation as a continuous work of God. God has not only made the world but supports and sustains it. God's relationship to the world is through **his word of power.** God is one whose relationship to the world is personal, taking the form of speech.

1:3b. The central theme of the entire work appears for the first time in **when he had made purification for sins.** The author seeks to show how Jesus Christ fulfills the Levitical priesthood of the Old Testament. Thus he brings to light the reality which the priesthood foreshadows. But in this passage the author's chief concern is to assert the glory of Christ. When he finished his work of purification, he achieved authority and power, symbolized by the image of **the right hand of the Majesty.**

1:4. The statement that the Son is **superior to angels** as well as the following paragraph make little sense to us. Angels play no significant role in our thought. But in the first century reference to angels was not speculation about heaven's population. It was concern for revelation. God was so remote and exalted that revelation became possible only if heavenly messengers were at hand to convey God's message. In the thought of the rabbis, angels were the intermediaries who brought the law. It is in this light that we must see the author's concern. Jesus is greater than the angels. He has a **name . . . more excellent:** the Son. He does a more perfect work: the fulfillment of Old Testament prophecy, including the prophetic institution of sacrifice. He brings the perfect and complete revelation, the disclosure of God's love in the cross.

II. The Identity of Jesus Christ (1:5–4:13)

After the eloquent statement of his theme, the author moves into a lengthy theological statement (1:5–10:18). This consists of two main sections, each having passages of exhortation which apply the message to the life and situation of the readers. This first main section deals with the question: Who is Jesus Christ? The author has already indicated his convictions on this question. In the opening thematic statement he has given a series of descriptions. He now proceeds to support and defend these claims. First he compares Jesus to the angels, the heavenly beings who are the bearers of divine revelation. Then Jesus is compared to Moses, the mediator of the covenant given by God to Israel after the exodus deliverance. The author's practical interests appear clearly in the way he makes an application of his theological statement in two sections of exhortation (2:1-4 and 3:6*b*–4:13). These contain practical reflections on the meaning of Christ's preeminence to the believer.

A. SUPERIORITY TO THE ANGELS (1:5–2:18)

This first section has three parts:

(1) a demonstration from scripture that Jesus is superior to the angels (1:5-14);

(2) an exhortation to take this fact seriously (2:1-4);

(3) a summary discussion of Jesus' work in salvation (2:5-18).

1:5-14. *Demonstration from Scripture.* The superiority of the Son over the angels is shown by seven quotations from the Old Testament. Five of these assert the preeminence of the Son in his unique relationship to the Father. The other two stress the servant function of the angels and their obligation to worship the Son.

1:5a. The first quotation is from Psalm 2:7. This was a "royal" psalm, a song used in the enthronement of a king in Israel. **"Thou art my Son, today I have begotten thee"** was a legal formula used in the ceremony of adoption in ancient Semitic countries. The father pronounced the formula to the child whom he was adopting, with witnesses present to certify the fact. The child thus became the son and heir of his father. In ancient law no distinction was made between natural and adopted children.

11

The use of the formula in the enthronement ceremony stressed such a relationship between God and the king. Here the author sees the enthronement ceremony as a prophetic event pointing forward to the coming of the true King. Thus the words of the psalm are supremely fitting in the enthronement of the Messiah. In the Lukan tradition the baptism of Jesus is interpreted as a coronation (Luke 3:22).

1:5b. The second quotation is from II Samuel 7:14. This was a prophecy of Nathan concerning the establishment of David's kingdom. David was the greatest king for the Jews and a favorite prophetic symbol. He had been called from his tasks as a shepherd to become the shepherd of his people, and God had promised that his throne would be established forever. From the long and moving speech of Nathan the author chooses the words that assert the father-son relationship of God and the Davidic king. Here David is treated as a prophetic figure who finds his true place as a preparation for the great King.

1:6. The third quotation does not appear in the Hebrew text. It comes from a Septuagint expansion of the conclusion to the Song of Moses (Deuteronomy 32:43). In the Septuagint context **him** clearly means God. Here the author views it as referring to the Son.

1:7. Psalm 104:4 praises the greatness of God, who uses creation as royal regalia, making "winds thy messengers, fire and flame [lightning] thy ministers." The Hebrew text is ambiguous, however. At least two other translations are possible—one of which, as found in the Septuagint, is followed here. The author uses this quotation as a kind of stepping stone to the last three citations. The meaning is: this is what God says about the angels, or messengers, but what is said about the Son is far greater.

1:8-9. Psalm 45:6-7 is another of the royal psalms declaring the honor and favor of God to the anointed king of Israel. This psalm stresses the permanence of the **kingdom,** the king's love of **righteousness,** and the consequent graciousness of God.

1:10-12. The quotation from Psalm 102:25-27 is notable in that the psalm is addressed to Yahweh, the God of the covenant. But the Septuagint's translation of this divine name by a word meaning "Lord" enables the author to apply the text to Jesus, who is the Lord from the Christian viewpoint. Thus understood, the passage asserts Jesus' activity in the creation of the world. It adds that the creation is transient but the creator is eternal.

The early Christian conviction that Jesus is Lord does not rest solely on such debatable interpretations of the Old Testament, but on a total interpretation of what he did, what he said, and what he was. Many different lines of Old Testament interpretation converge on this conviction. This passage from Psalm 102 did not create the conviction. Yet once the conviction of Christ's lordship existed, it was natural that passages like this should be used to expound the meaning of his status as Lord.

1:13-14. Psalm 110:1, another of the royal psalms, forms the climax of the series of quotations. It speaks of the exaltation of the king to the **right hand** of honor, power, and majesty. Though the psalm was used in the enthronement of kings of Israel, it was historically true of none of them. Its truth is prophetic: in the victory of Jesus the Son the validity of earlier enthronements is established. Through his obedience to death he won a victory over his **enemies** and now reigns. By way of contrast the angels, great and powerful as they are, have been sent forth as servants **for the sake of those** whom God seeks to save.

2:1-4. *An Exhortation.* Chapter 2 opens with one of the several sections of exhortation throughout the book. The author evidently fears that his readers are in danger of drifting away from the message concerning Jesus Christ. He urges them to hold fast to it for two reasons:

(1) because of the judgment that awaits those who neglect it;

(2) because the message has been **declared . . . by the Lord** and affirmed **by signs and . . . miracles** worked by God.

2:2-3. The **message** of the old covenant **declared by angels was valid.** Everyone who transgressed it came under the judgment of God. This is the premise which the author and his readers share. But if this message is valid and brings judgment to those who disobey it, how much more serious it is to ignore the message brought by the Son! This message was given by

Jesus himself. He is the greatest of the prophets. He speaks the word of God with authority, not simply as one who hands on a tradition. **Those who heard him,** the apostles, transmitted his message through their preaching, bringing it to people like those addressed here.

2:4. Their testimony was not by words alone, however. It was accompanied by miracles and **by gifts of the Holy Spirit.** The early church did not regard miracles as objects of faith or as ends in themselves but as confirmation of the testimony given by Christ and his apostles. The object of faith is Christ himself. The miracles are signs which command attention but point beyond themselves to the message and mission of Christ.

The danger of the people addressed here is not heresy or immorality but neglect and carelessness. They are in peril of drifting away from the word of God. Judgment will overtake them—not because of gross wickedness, but because they **neglect** the salvation offered them in Jesus Christ.

2:5-18. *Jesus' Work in Salvation.* The author now resumes his theological argument. Christ's superiority to the angels is urged not only because scripture testifies to it (1:5-14) but also because of what Christ was and did during the days of his flesh.

2:6-9. Psalm 8 speaks of the wonder of human beings as compared with the majesty of the heavens. God has made them only a little less than divine and subjected all things to them. In quoting the Septuagint version of Psalm 8:4-6 the author underlines the point that there are no exceptions to this statement. **Nothing** is **outside human control.** But, he adds, experience shows us that actually not everything is subject to humans. The fulfillment of this statement is therefore to be sought, not in human lives but in the career of **Jesus.** The Son was indeed **made lower than the angels** for a time. But **because of the suffering of death . . . for everyone** he is now **crowned with glory and honor.**

The mission of Jesus is thus seen as the fulfillment of the prophecy of Psalm 8. It is implied that he is the man of whom the psalmist writes, the true man whose career calls forth the wonder of the prophet. By his self-humiliation he identifies himself with humanity and becomes their representative. What he undergoes becomes the experience of the human race. What does not normally happen to humans occurs in the person of Jesus. Through God's goodness we have in our representative, Jesus Christ, the experience of God's crown of glory and honor.

2:10-11. The thought just hinted at is now developed. Christ is the pioneer of human **salvation.** He has gone out into the wilderness alone and broken the trail. This he has done by his identification of himself with all persons: **he is not ashamed to call them brethren.** But two other important ideas are also expressed. God's initiative in human salvation is emphasized. The Creator brings **many sons to glory** by making the Son **perfect through suffering.** Humanity's **origin** in God is also affirmed. Christ, **who sanctifies,** and humans who are sanctified by his work come from God. It is important to note that this author who stresses sin and the resulting separation from God also emphasizes our origin in God and the kinship of Christ with sinners.

2:12-13. Psalm 22:22 and Isaiah 8:17-18 are quoted here. This use of Old Testament quotations is again interesting and instructive. Jesus Christ, the fulfillment of God's revelation, is seen as speaking the prophetic word through the psalmist and the prophet. An interpreter today would begin with an examination of the passage in its literary and historical context and be concerned with what the words meant to their first readers. By contrast, the author has a vivid sense of being confronted by God's address both in Christ and in the Old Testament. Therefore he regards it as proper to read the word of prophecy in the light of its fulfillment. When he listens to the prophetic word of the Old Testament, it is really the voice of Christ that he is hearing. Thus he sees the prophet's identification of himself with the people of God as a prediction of Christ's identification of himself with men and women in his incarnation.

2:14-18. Those whom God seeks to save are **flesh and blood.** Therefore the Son takes the **same nature** on himself to enter into battle on behalf of his brothers and **deliver** them from **fear** and

bondage. In the first century the human plight in the world was seen as bondage to alien spirits. An important part of early Christian preaching portrays Christ as the one who overcomes the demonic host and their chief. His power to cast out demons, heal the sick, and cleanse lepers was seen as assurance that he had both authority and power to overcome the forces which held humanity in slavery.

The same imagery is used here, in a way which assumes that the language is familiar to the readers. The stress, however, is not so much on the victory of Christ as on the way he conformed himself **in every respect** to his brothers and sisters. He shared their plight in order that he might **make expiation for the sins.** As high priest he not only represents God's purpose in rescuing creation. He has undergone temptation and suffering and thus **is able to help** those who are subject to these afflictions.

B. SUPERIORITY TO MOSES (3:1-6*a*)

The blend of theological exposition and exhortation which characterizes this book is well illustrated in this section. Its purpose is to complete the demonstration of Christ's superiority to the law by showing that he is not only greater than the angels, the heavenly mediators of the law, but also greater than Moses, God's human instrument in the giving of the law. The opening verse, however, has the hortatory tone. This is picked up again in verse 6*b* and continued to 4:13 in a lengthy homily.

3:1. In this verse the author reminds his readers that they are **holy** through their relationship to Jesus Christ. They **share in a heavenly call.** The real center of their existence is not in their earthly circumstances but in God's will for their life. They are reminded to **consider Jesus,** who is both **apostle and high priest.** As apostle he represents the interests of the one who sent him. Here again the divine initiative in salvation is stressed. As high priest he mediates between God and humanity, bringing God's will to us and interceding for us in the divine presence.

Our confession does not refer to confession of sins, or to confession of faith in the sense of affirming a creed. In the New Testament the term "confession" refers to praise of God. It is the Christian's recognition that the proper attitude toward God is adoration and praise. The human failure and misery is that we are bound up in ourselves and give no thought to our creator. In Christ we recover the proper dimensions of our existence. We find our proper place in creation by joining in the chorus of praise ascending to God. Christians are first of all worshipers. The whole of their activity flows properly from a life of praise to God.

3:2-6a. Numbers 12:7 in the Septuagint speaks of "my servant Moses" as "faithful in all my house." Alluding to this, the author says that Christ was like Moses except that, instead of being a **servant, he was faithful over God's house as a son.** Therefore Christ is worthy of greater honor. Moses testified to matters which **were to be spoken later.** Christ is the content of these matters.

C. EXHORTATION (3:6b–4:13)

The exhortation compares the readers to Israel in the wilderness. It suggests that their lukewarmness will cause them **to fall away from the living God** and miss their deliverance.

3:6b-11. *The Household of God.* The author begins by recalling to his readers what they are—the **house,** or household, of God. This is one of the common biblical pictures of the people of God, the church. It emphasizes God's role as parent, the protective and nurturing care of God's family, the discipline which God imposes on the children, the love and affection which God displays, and the intimate relationship which they enjoy. They do not exist as slaves or as servants but as members of the family. They move about in the home with confidence and freedom.

3:6b. A conditional clause is a reminder that the family relationship is not automatic. It is only as we **hold fast our confidence and pride in our hope** that we remain God's household. **Confidence** implies the confident boldness of children in their own home. **Pride** might be expressed rather as exultant rejoicing or even boasting. God has provided the church with great riches. But the church can experience poverty if it becomes absentminded and overlooks what God has done. The author seeks to rouse his readers to a state of confident boldness in which they will rejoice in what God has done for them.

3:7-11. This quotation from Psalm 95 invites God's people to come into the divine presence to worship. It reminds them that God is the creator of all things and that the whole creation lives by God's bounty. Most important, the Lord is their God and they are God's people, the sheep of the pasture. It is only after this recital of God's goodness and the invitation to worship that the solemn warning is given. Israel **in the wilderness** was surrounded by the evidences of God's goodness and care, and yet many of the people missed the encounter with God. Their problem was not the gross carnal appetites but "hardness of heart"—or, as we might put it, insensitivity. They simply had too many things on their minds to heed the presence of God among them.

3:12-19. *The Failure of Israel.* The exhortation becomes specific. Be alert lest history repeat itself. The essence of sin is idolatry, the refusal to worship the true God. This is also the **deceitfulness of sin.** As long as we avoid the more dramatic sins and crimes we consider ourselves sound. But the subtlety of sin is that it puts something—sometimes something good—in the place of God. "Original" sin is to put one's own preferences before the will of God. As a result all the structures of life are distorted and misshapen. The congregation here addressed was most likely an orderly and respectable group, unmarred by crimes or vices. But in their complacent respectability they are in danger of losing God. What they need most of all is the recovery of a sensitivity to God's work and presence among them.

3:14. For we share in Christ implies that an action in the past has made us effectual partakers of Christ—**if only we hold . . . firm** the solid foundation we have been given. Christians' standing is not the product of decision, obedience, or theological insight. They stand on the basis of God's deed in Jesus Christ and God's act in uniting them to Christ. They can render this ineffectual by drifting away from it through preoccupation or carelessness. But even the one who has drifted can recover the center again. One can find anew the great event that gives meaning and perspective to life, and build again on the foundation laid by God.

3:16-19. Three rhetorical questions focus the author's concern: Who **heard and yet were rebellious?** With whom was God **provoked forty years?** Whom did God forbid to **enter his rest?** It was the very people who experienced the deliverance of the exodus, the notable sign of God's love and care. The parallel is an instructive one for early Christians. For Israel the great emblem of God's mercy was the exodus. Here was the ground of their assurance that God had called them to be the chosen people. For Christians the decisive act of God is Jesus Christ, who is the sign of God's mercy to creatures. But the exodus generation drifted into **unbelief** and lost the promise. It is equally easy for Christians to miss the significance of Christ and to idle away into unbelief. That the author regarded this as a real possibility for his contemporaries is shown by the fact that he continues his exhortation for most of the next chapter.

4:1-10. *The Danger of Failure Today.* In 3:18 the sabbath **rest** has been mentioned. This theme is now picked up and developed. The sabbath was central to Jewish piety both in Palestine and among those who lived in the Gentile world. It was a sign that looked both backward and forward. It looked back to the creation of the world and was an enduring reminder to Jews that their God was no provincial deity but the God of the entire earth. It also served as a memorial of the covenant. It recalled to the Jews their vocation as the people of God and their destiny to bring the knowledge of the Lord's name to all peoples.

It looked forward to the rest that God promised to the people. Its weekly observance was a reminder that though Israel was small, often despised and persecuted, its future was with God. And just as **God rested** from labor on the sabbath, so a weary and discouraged Israel should one day enter into God's rest. The Promised Land seemed to one generation the fulfillment of the hope of rest. But the people were unwilling to take the risk of trusting God, and for their lack of faith lost the promise.

Underlying the thought of this section is the idea that the sabbath is prophetic in character. Its meaning is not exhausted in the backward reference to creation and the covenant. It has also a forward reference to a yet unfinished work of God. Jesus Christ is the realization of this forward thrust. The prophetic work of God comes to completion in him. Those who are in him, those who have faith, therefore already take part through this faith in God's sabbath rest. And faith is decisive. Its presence means a real participation in the fulfillment of God's plan. Its absence makes the message of no benefit to those who hear because they do not receive it with faith. And here is the major concern of the book. Good news came to Israel, but because faith was lacking there was no entry into **God's rest.**

The abiding peril of the Christian church is the same. The good news is proclaimed, but unless it is received by faith the promise remains ineffectual. Israel's history is one of God's goodness and human disobedience. But God speaks of another day. In Christ God offers once more the gift of rest to those who believe. There **remains a sabbath rest for the people of God.** Those who have faith in Christ enter into that rest.

4:11-13. *The Word of God.* The exhortation comes to an eloquent climax. **Let us . . . strive to enter that rest,** that no one repeat the history of Israel's **disobedience.**

Faith is an active thing. This is so partly because the **word of God,** which calls it forth, is also **living and active.** Since the invention of printing there has been the constant temptation to think of the word of God as a body of doctrine or a book. For the Scriptures the word of God is the word which God addresses to the creation. It is the word which God speaks through the prophet, making the divine will known to people. It is the word of power by which God created and sustains the world. It is the word of apostolic preaching, declaring the good news of what God has done in Jesus Christ. It is Christ himself as the sum and substance of God's speech. In all these uses it is the personal encounter with the God who honors creatures by addressing them with the demand for responsibility and the offer of life.

The word which God addresses to creatures establishes effective communication. It penetrates into the innermost recesses of the personality, **piercing to the division of soul and spirit.** It leaves no place to hide from God's presence. The prophets impressed their contemporaries in this way. An encounter with Jesus Christ was for many a similar experience of being opened up to oneself and to his searching eyes. One reason that unbelief remains so constant a threat in the Christian community is our tendency to live in our self-chosen deceptions. But we cannot hide from God. The peril of our encounter with God is that of being stripped of all evasions and defenses—of being compelled to see ourselves with clarity and honesty.

III. THE ACCOMPLISHMENT OF JESUS CHRIST (4:14–10:18)

The second main section of the book discusses what Jesus Christ accomplished in his mission. Exposition and exhortation are mingled. The preacher follows hard on the heels of the theologian. The author first sets out his view that Christ is priest after the order of Melchizedek (4:14–5:10; see below on 5:11-14 and 7:1-28). Then follows a lengthy exhortation in which rebuke, warning, and encouragement are mingled together (5:11–6:20). He next asserts the superiority of the priesthood of Jesus to that of the Levites (7:1-28). Finally he offers a summary discussion of Jesus' ministry as high priest (8:1–10:18).

A. HIGH PRIEST AFTER THE ORDER OF MELCHIZEDEK (4:14–5:10)

4:14-16. *A Transition.* These verses summarize the preceding exhortation and lead into the new section, which discusses the priestly activity of the Son.

4:14a. In Israelite worship the high priest **passed through** the veil separating the most holy place in the temple once each year as he made atonement for the sins of the people. Christians have a **great high priest who has passed through the heavens,** fulfilling what is symbolized in the entry of the holy of holies and coming into the presence of God. He is identified explicitly as **Jesus, the Son of God.** This identification holds the earthly and the heavenly names together. It points to the fact that he combines in this remarkable way an ordinary life as a human being with an extraordinary calling as God's high priest.

4:14b-15. Since our personal history involves this great event and includes the person of Jesus, the great high priest, we should **hold fast our confession.** This is both a testimony of our faith in and loyalty to God and also a song of praise to God's marvelous acts of redemption. The readers are urged to remember the meaning of their experience and not to lose it through inattention or neglect. The author supports his exhortation with a reason. Our high priest is not inaccessible. He is one who has endured the struggles of human life, who knows what temptations human beings face and can therefore be sympathetic to their problems. His sinlessness is not the spotlessness of an object sealed from contamination but a human achievement. Jesus was really **tempted** but remained in obedience and fellowship with the Father. Thus he is without sin.

4:16. Because he has shared our experience we can have **confidence** as we approach the **throne,** a symbol of his triumph and authority. It is moreover the throne of **grace.** The chief characteristic of the rule of Christ is that it is gracious. He rules, not through the power of armies, but through the power of grace. God is strong enough and secure enough in ruling that graciousness can be shown even to enemies. Because the throne is occupied by one whose strength is graciousness, those who draw near may confidently expect **to receive mercy . . . in time of need.**

5:1-10. *The Priestly Qualifications of Jesus.* Priests are chosen **to act on behalf** of their fellows. They have the responsibility **to**

offer gifts and sacrifices to God for both their own sins and those of others. Because they know what human life is like they should be able to deal sympathetically with others, even with those who are **ignorant** or are wandering astray. The position is not one which men seek for themselves. The priest should be **called by God, just as Aaron was.**

5:5-6. Jesus fulfills the above qualifications. He did not seek the position but held it by divine appointment. His appointment came in the divine declaration of two royal psalms quoted here (2:7; 110:4). How these verses gave Jesus the assurance of his calling to be high priest is not indicated. The Synoptic gospels quote the first as a part of Jesus' experience at his baptism, and it may be that the author assumes the knowledge of traditions such as this among his readers. His use of the passages suggests his conviction that the voice of God speaking in the psalmists reaches its proper objective in the person of the man Jesus, who thus recognizes himself as the one divinely appointed to the task of high priesthood.

Our historical approach to the Old Testament and our preoccupation with psychological questions such as how Jesus came to know himself as Messiah and high priest raise for us questions which did not occur to the author or his readers. It was enough for them that God spoke in the Old Testament. They held that his message was delivered to the right person when it reached Jesus, who did not aspire to the duties of high priest, but accepted them when he was named by God.

5:7. The qualification of identity with the people was fulfilled by Jesus in his life of temptation and prayer. His fellowship with God and obedience to the divine will were not given at the outset and then sealed throughout his life. They were achieved through strenuous effort and acceptance of suffering. **Loud cries and tears** may be a reference to the Passion, but shows at least the Semitic coloration of the account. Compared with the composure of Socrates in face of death, or the Stoic fortitude so much admired in the western tradition, people of the Middle East were far less restrained in the expression of their emotions. Jesus wept as he contemplated Jerusalem (Luke 19:41). He showed anger at the harshness of his opponents (Mark 3:5). He manifested strong emotion in Gethsemane (Mark 14:33). But he also showed remarkable self-control in the face of the disbelief of his disciples (Mark 5:31), the crowd (Mark 5:40), and the authorities (Mark 14:61).

The main point, however, is not that Jesus was exposed to great strains and sufferings but that in them he turned in prayer to God. **He was heard for his godly fear** and received deliverance from his afflictions. This was not the deliverance of escape, but the power to endure what came upon him.

5:8-10. Even though **he was a Son,** Jesus **learned obedience** in the school of suffering. Through it he **became the source of eternal salvation.** The language echoes that of Philippians 2:9 and stresses again the initiative of God in the work of Jesus Christ. He was heard, **being made perfect,** being designated by God a high priest. It is the Son who obeys, who suffers, but his obedience is the expression of the Father's will that humanity should be redeemed. The perfection mentioned here is not that of a painting or statue which satisfies all the criteria of artistic excellence. It is the perfection of that which is adapted to its purpose. The author's stress is not on the moral excellence of Jesus but on the fact that he submitted to whatever was necessary for the accomplishment of his work.

B. Exhortations (5:11–6:20)

5:11-14. *A Rebuke.* The previous section concludes with a second reference to priesthood **after the order of Melchizedek** (cf. verse 6). This figure is mentioned only in passing in the Old Testament and is a puzzle to us (see below on 7:1-28). It apparently puzzled people in the first century too. The author admits that he has **much to say** on the subject and great difficulty in making it clear. He opens a long section of exhortation by asserting that the difficulty lies in the deficiencies of his readers. They **have become dull of hearing.** They ought by now to be teaching others, but are in need of learning the ABC's of God's word. At a time when they should be eating **solid food** they are still behaving like infants and living on **milk.** They have not yet acquired the ability to distinguish between good and evil. Therefore they cannot be dealt with as mature people.

This section adds to our knowledge of both the readers and the author. We can again see that the peril of those here addressed is not immorality or heresy. They are simply inattentive—Christians taking themselves for granted, neither anxious nor excited, but nevertheless in danger of losing their faith. They have not advanced in their understanding of the gospel. Christian service has not equipped them to discriminate among values. They present the embarrassing sight of adults who are still bottle fed—an image with just enough humor to ease the bite of the author's rebuke.

The author shows himself again as a theologian who is also a preacher, interweaving theology and exhortation throughout the book. His exposition is for the sake of obedience. Clarification is never enough. He insists on involvement. His intense moral earnestness is barely relieved by the seasoning of humor—which, however, is not permitted to disturb the exalted and elegant style.

6:1-8. *A Warning.* Rebuke is followed by warning. Complacency and indifference will end in the judgment of God. Proper and respectable church people do not realize the seriousness of their situation. They are actually on the verge of nailing Christ to the cross all over again.

6:1-3. The opening verses are tantalizing in their vagueness. It is clear that the ABC's are to be left behind for growth toward **maturity.** It is clear that the list comprises a kind of catechism. But the context that would enable us to grasp the meaning and relationship of the terms is not supplied. The list apparently includes elements familiar to the readers, elements which they are inclined to interpret as the whole of the Christian religion. Some of the terms offer no difficulty. **Repentance from dead works** (works which have no life-giving power) **. . . faith toward God . . . resurrection of the dead . . . eternal judgment** sound like familiar elements in Christian teaching to us.

But **ablutions**—literally "baptisms" (note the plural)—sound more like the ceremonial practices of Judaism than anything familiar in the Christian tradition. **Laying on of hands** is also a familiar Jewish practice. It was taken over by Christians in connection with the forgiveness of sins, healing, and the bestowal of the Holy Spirit. Whatever the details may mean, the message of the total passage is clear. Christians must move on from beginnings to maturity. Here the author identifies himself with his readers: **this we will do if God permits.**

6:4-6. The danger of not moving on to maturity is that of sliding into **apostasy.** Here are some of the sharpest and most solemn words of the letter, indeed of scripture as a whole. The denial of the possibility of a second **repentance** has troubled many readers, causing some to refuse allowing lapsed believers to be reinstated in the church. It is not clear whether the reason a second repentance is considered impossible is theological— the will of God, or psychological—the hardening of the human heart. The distinction is one which would not occur to the author but which is inevitable for modern readers.

Tasted the goodness of the word of God implies, not sampling, but a genuine experience of the reality. **Powers of the age to come** is common language in the early church, which believed that in Jesus Christ and his church the powers of the age to come were already at work. God's future is already present where the gospel is preached and believed. Apostasy is to **crucify the Son of God.** Those who have once bowed before him in worship now join in bringing about his death and offering him to the **contempt** of bystanders.

6:7-8. The image of the cultivated field is common among the Old Testament prophets. Israel is God's farm or vineyard, and God expects a harvest. The field which does not bring a harvest is worthless. Its yield of **thorns and thistles** is only fit **to be burned.**

6:9-12. *Encouragement.* The warning is followed by words of encouragement. The solemn warning was necessary: apostasy follows complacency. But the author holds out **better things** for his readers. God will not **overlook** the evidence of genuine faith among them—faith shown in their **work,** in their past and present deeds of mercy to the **saints,** and in the **love** which motivated these acts.

We can be confident in the sovereign goodness of God, who has brought **salvation** in Christ and has also awakened faith among men and women. If matters depend on us, the doom portrayed above would be the outcome. But since matters depend on God, there is ground for hope for the future of God's children. And here again is the paradox. Because salvation is God's work, therefore do not be **sluggish,** but hold your **hope** firmly to **the end** and become **imitators of those who through faith and patience inherit the promises.** Human cunning says: if it is all of God, then we can relax. Faith says: since it is all God's work, therefore hang on patiently to the end. Note that faith and patience do not earn their reward, but faith and patience inherit the promises. One inherits what someone else has worked to amass. The promise is a free and generous offer, not the result of haggling.

6:13-20. *Assurance.* Encouragement is followed by assurance. God's deeds are recounted as a basis for the confidence just expressed. Our hope is not in the voltage generated by our faith, nor in the reputation earned by our good works, but solely in the character of the one who has made the promise. **God made a promise to Abraham** and confirmed it by an **oath.** God had made the promise earlier, and when Abraham was willing to offer up even his son at God's command, the promise was confirmed (Genesis 22:16-17). God condescends to the human craving for assurance and gives **two unchangeable things,** a word of **promise** and an **oath.** Thus God makes the divine will unmistakably clear and firm.

It is interesting to note the difference of accent in Paul's reading of this same Old Testament passage in Galatians 3:6-9. Paul stresses that the old covenant was also a religion of grace, that Abraham obtained the promise through faith. Here the emphasis falls on the faithfulness of God, a faithfulness underlined by his oath.

6:19a. The long exhortation moves to its close with a pair of vivid pictures. Since God cannot lie, we refugees have strong encouragement to grasp firmly the hope which has been extended to us. God offers the hope to us. Since God is dependable, we ought to reach out and take it. This hope is a **sure and steadfast anchor of the soul**—that is, for our life. **Soul** in the Bible is not some ethereal inner substance, but a way of expressing what we call person, or personality. Christian hope keeps one securely anchored in port. It gives stability, poise, confidence. It does this because of the surpassing reliability of the one who holds out the hope.

6:19b-20. The second picture is taken from the Old Testament tabernacle. The Christian's **hope** does not linger in its outer courts. It enters into the holy of holies, **the inner shrine . . . where Jesus has gone** to be our **forerunner.** This is not the tabernacle in the wilderness nor the later temple but their counterpart in heaven, of which they are only shadows. The Christian hope, being fixed in Christ, enters into the realm of the real. Hope is thus a kind of participation in the reality hoped for because of the steadfastness of God who guarantees the hope. With the closing phrase the exhortation comes to a well-turned conclusion. This both restates the subject previously discussed and resumes the argument interrupted by the hortatory section.

C. The Superiority of Jesus' Priesthood to the Levitical Priesthood (7:1-28)

The closing words of chapter 6 are a quotation from Psalm 110:4. They reintroduce the figure of Melchizedek (cf. 5:6, 10), who is mentioned elsewhere only in Genesis 14:17-20. That such a shadowy figure should serve in a theological argument seems strange to us. Even stranger is the way the Old Testament reference to him is interpreted. But unfamiliar as the interpretative principles may be to us, the argument of the chapter is clear. There is a priesthood older than that of Levi (verses 1-3). In the encounter of Abraham and Melchizedek it is also established as superior (verses 4-10). Since the Levitical priesthood is plainly inadequate, the priesthood is changed (verses 11-14). Christ appears in the line of Melchizedek. He introduces a better hope (verses 15-19), which is guaranteed by an oath (verses 20-22). This priesthood is permanent (verses 23-25) and the sacrifice of Christ is offered once for all (verses 26-28).

7:1-3. *An Older Priesthood.* The story in Genesis 14 is summarized briefly, with stress on the fact that Abraham gave a **tenth** of the plunder to Melchizedek. The significance of his name and title is then pointed out. Melchizedek is related to the story of salvation as **king of righteousness** and **king of peace.** Finally rabbinic principles of interpretation are applied to stress his resemblance to the **Son of God.**

Verse 3 is only an argument from silence, and is not particularly persuasive. But the rabbis believed it was not only what God said in scripture that was important but also what God did not say. The absence of vital statistics and of reference to parents is therefore used to heighten the mysterious significance of Melchizedek in the unfolding of salvation history. Having made his point the author leaves it quickly, since his interest is not so much in Melchizedek as in the priesthood which he represents.

7:4-10. *A Superior Priesthood.* Melchizedek blessed Abraham and received tithes from him. Since the greater blesses the lesser, Abraham concurred in the superiority of Melchizedek.

The descendants of Levi exact tithes from the people of Israel in accordance with the Mosaic law. Levi, in the person of his great-grandfather Abraham, actually offered **tithes** to Melchizedek. This argument is less clear to us than to a people who stressed the continuity between generations and the subordination of the younger to the older. Verse 8 reasserts the point of verse 3. Since nothing is said in scripture about the death of Melchizedek, the ancient interpreter can conclude that the silence is deliberate and meaningful. Melchizedek still lives; he continues a priest forever.

7:11-14. *The Priesthood Changed.* It has already been shown that Jesus is high priest (4:14–5:10). But why another priesthood in the order of Melchizedek if the Levitical priesthood was adequate? The fact that another priestly order has been established shows that the priesthood of Aaron and his descendants did not achieve perfection. But a **change in the priesthood** means also a **change in the law.** This becomes clear when it is recalled that Jesus the high priest comes from the tribe of **Judah,** and that **Moses said nothing** authorizing priests from that tribe. Thus from the change of priesthood the author argues back to a change in the law which establishes the priesthood. All of this discussion seems to us involved and obscure because we do not share the presuppositions about covenant, law, priesthood, and sacrifice which underlie it. Further, the logical progression seems to us not direct but crablike, sidling from one point to another.

7:15-19. *Christ in the Line of Melchizedek.* It is encouraging to note that even the author's contemporaries may have had difficulties with the paragraph above. To make matters clearer to them he introduces two illustrations. First, the high priest is here. He is Jesus Christ. He has become priest, not by birth into the priestly tribe, but by virtue of a **life** which has overcome death. His high priesthood is established by his fulfillment of a priestly mission and confirmed by the prophetic word in Psalm 110:4. Thus the career of Jesus and the testimony of the scripture converge on the conclusion that he is God's high priest, not in the order of Levi, but in that of Melchizedek.

7:18-19. The second illustration is an appeal to experience. The law was weak and useless. It failed to bring about perfection; therefore it has been **set aside.** In its place a **better hope is introduced** which enables people to come into the divine presence.

7:20-22. *An Oath as Guaranty.* Another distinctive mark of the new covenant is that an oath accompanied its establishment. Priests in the Levitical order **took their office without an oath.** The high priest of the new covenant **was addressed with an oath.** Through the prophetic scriptures God assured him that his appointment was firm and unchangeable. God is not going to change his mind. Jesus is therefore the **surety of a better covenant.** Behind him and his mission stand the determination of God, who is bound with an oath and a firmly established promise.

7:23-25. _A Permanent Priesthood._ The numerous priests of the old covenant died and had to be replaced. But Christ lives **for ever** and therefore **holds his priesthood permanently.** At this point the preacher breaks through the involved chain of theological reasoning with a homiletical point. Because Christ lives forever he exercises his intercessory mission permanently. He therefore **is able for all time to save those who draw near to God through him.** Christ's victory over death is an event in both the temporal and eternal worlds. It is a theological affirmation with many consequences, one of which is stressed here. The Christian does not need many deliverers. Christ is quite adequate **since he always lives to make intercession for them.**

7:26-28. _A Sacrifice Once for All._ An earlier passage emphasized Christ's human experience, which equipped him to deal sympathetically with weakness. Here a complementary aspect of his career is stressed. He is the exceptional one—consecrated to God, beyond reproach, without stain. By the quality of his life he is effectively set apart from sinful humans. Through his victory over death he is **exalted above the heavens.** His uniqueness sets him apart from other high priests. They must **offer sacrifices daily,** for their own sins before those of others. Christ's sacrifice is a once-for-all offering of himself to God. Others are appointed high priests by the law in their human **weakness.** He has been appointed as **a Son . . . made perfect for ever.** With this catalog of qualities in view it is important to note that he is our high priest. Great and wonderful as he is, it is the more remarkable that he is God's gift to us.

D. THE MINISTRY OF JESUS AS HIGH PRIEST (8:1–10:18)

The fourth section interprets the work of Jesus as high priest in the heavenly sanctuary (8:1-5). This implies a new covenant

(8:6-13). It offers a new sacrifice (9:1-14) which fulfills the promise of the new covenant (9:15–10:18). Its thought is a combination of two ideas:

(1) Platonic ideas, in which the reality of the heavenly is contrasted with the shadowy character of the earthly.

(2) Biblical ideas which stress the forward movement of the purpose of God toward fulfillment. Thus ideas taken from the world of space are combined with those derived from the realm of time in a remarkable theological synthesis.

8:1-5. *Jesus' Ministry in the Heavenly Sanctuary.* The author seems aware that his previous argument is difficult and complex. He now proceeds to restate it in a summary way. The word translated **point** can also be rendered "pith" or "substance." We have a high priest who possesses power. He ministers in the tabernacle established by God, not by humans. The risen Jesus has not gone into retirement but continues to serve as high priest in the heavenly sanctuary. The author uses an array of images from Jewish theology. **Seated at the right hand** is not to be taken literally. The Jew of ancient times was well aware that his scriptures were filled with images or metaphors. The right hand is the place of honor, preferment, and power. The joining of this image with that of the **throne of the Majesty** stresses again that the power of Jesus derives from God the Father and that it is his through his carrying out of the Father's purpose.

Majesty reflects the Jewish reluctance to pronounce the name of God, a custom rooted in profound reverence for the transcendent God. A similar usage is reflected in expressions such as "kingdom of heaven" (Matthew 5:3) and "right hand of Power" (Matthew 26:64).

8:2. The reference to the **true tent** suggests that the author is not interested primarily in the Jerusalem temple but in its predecessor, the tabernacle. He may share the idea of Stephen who regarded the building of the temple as a mistake (Acts 7). The tabernacle in the wilderness seems to him a better symbol of the voluntary relationship of God to the covenant people, as well as the character of the people as pilgrims. Or he may be writing at a time when emotions aroused by mention of the temple destroyed by the Romans might divert readers from his argument (see Introduction). Whether we think of tabernacle or temple, we are concerned with an earthly structure which symbolizes a heavenly reality. Jesus, the great high priest, serves, not in an earthly shrine, but in the very presence of God.

Since this is true, the earthly sanctuary with its rituals and sacrifices is no longer important. There was a time when people related themselves to God through tabernacle or temple. The ministry of Jesus, however, has changed that situation. People now should relate themselves to God through the new way opened to them through Christ's high-priestly work. Life in Christ opens new possibilities. It offers a better covenant, better promises, through the Man who lives forever.

8:3-5. What follows seems difficult to us, partly because the author's logic differs from ours. But it is even more difficult because we do not share his presuppositions about worship and sacrifice. High priesthood is established for the offering of **gifts and sacrifices.** Therefore Christ as priest should also have an offering to make. We expect now a discussion of Christ's sacrificial activity. Instead this is postponed until 9:11. A new line of argument appears in its place, pointing out the inadequacy of the covenant with Israel. It is introduced by pointing out that if Christ **were on earth, he would not be a priest at all.** The earthly sanctuary was served by priests of the house of Levi. Jesus was not even of the priestly family. But the sanctuary which they served is not the true sanctuary. It is rather a **copy** of it, an earthly **shadow** cast by the heavenly reality.

The quotation from Exodus 25:40 is used to prove the secondary character of the tabernacle. Moses' instructions were to follow the **pattern** disclosed to him on Mt. Sinai. We tend to read this text as meaning Moses was shown plans for the tabernacle. The author takes it to mean that Moses was given a glimpse of the heavenly reality and instructed to pattern the earthly sanctuary after it.

8:6-13. *The New Covenant.* The ministry of Christ is **more excellent** than the ministry of the old covenant. It mediates a

better covenant and is based on **better promises.** Here we
return to the groundwork laid in the opening chapters. Jesus is
the Son, and he is high priest in the distinctive order of
Melchizedek. Without further argument on this point the
author now turns, not to the superiority of the new, but to the
inferiority of the old. He establishes this point with a quotation
from Jeremiah 31:31-34. Scripture itself testifies to the
imperfections of the old covenant. It looks longingly toward a
future day when God will establish a new and better
relationship. If the old covenant had been perfect, there would
have been no reason for another.

8:8-13. The passage from Jeremiah makes clear that it was not
the covenant that was to blame. God **finds fault** with the chosen
people. Israel's disobedience and waywardness ruined the old
covenant. Therefore God has to take other measures to achieve
the goal of fellowship with the people. God will put **laws into
their minds** and **hearts,** so that all will be full of the knowledge of
the divine will. In the light of this vision the old covenant is seen
as inadequate, even **obsolete, . . . ready to vanish away.** At this
point we return from examination of the old to an exposition of
the offering brought by Jesus the priest.

9:1-14. *Old and New Sacrifices Contrasted.* The old may be
obsolete, but it still has continuity with the new. As a shadow of
the new it offers itself for edifying comparisons, which are drawn
in detail. Verses 1-10 discuss the earthly priesthood. They
describe the place where it functions, its way of approach to
God, its sacrifice, and an evaluation of its work. Verses 11-14 set
forth somewhat more briefly the priesthood of Christ. They
follow precisely the same pattern: the place of his ministry, his
way of approach to God, his sacrifice, and an evaluation of his
work.

9:1-5. The description of the tabernacle is quite detailed.
However, it differs significantly from the account in Exodus
25:10-40, which does not locate Aaron's rod or the urn
containing the manna within the **Holy of Holies.** Whether the
author is following another tradition or altering details for
symbolic reasons—or is not especially concerned about exact

correspondence with the Exodus account—is not possible to say. He sketches the two main parts of the tabernacle clearly. The chief furnishings are described. In the **Holy Place** are the **lampstand** and **table.** In the **Holy of Holies** are the **altar of incense** and **ark of the covenant** containing the memorials of the exodus deliverance, with the figures of the **cherubim** above it.

9:6-7a. The approach to God is now presented. The priests are busy with their prescribed duties each day in the **outer tent.** The inner tent is entered **but once a year** and only by the high priest in the offering for the people's sins. This stresses the difficulty of access to God under the old covenant and the importance of the priestly office. Without a priest expiation of sins is impossible.

9:7b. In the mention of the sacrifice three points may be noted:

(1) The priest offers **blood,** which for Hebrew thought is the seat of life. For us it may suggest that in sacrifice the guilt of the worshiper is transferred to an animal which is put to death in place of the person. But biblical thought sees sacrifice rather as the offering of one's own life. This is symbolized by the identification of the worshiper and the sacrifice in the laying on of hands. When the prophets speak against the abuse of sacrifice, they are attacking the mistaken notion that one can barter with or buy God off. Understood in the context of prophetic religion, sacrifice is a profound expression of one's basic relationship to God. It is a recognition of God's ultimate claim and a way of offering one's life to God.

(2) The priest offers sacrifice **for himself** as well as the people. He does not stand aside from the people but in their midst. His priestly character is enhanced by his awareness that he shares the frailty of his fellows. This aspect has been stressed previously in outlining Jesus' credentials as high priest (5:1-10).

(3) The priest offers for the people's **errors.** This is a reminder that in the old covenant there was no way to atone for deliberate sins. Sacrifice provides a way of atonement for sins of weakness but not for sins done "with a high hand." Sacrifice is efficacious for those who live within the covenant. It is only for

those who stand before God as God's people. It is not an automatic or magic device to provide cleansing for the impious or careless. Even in the old covenant one's relationship to God was personal and responsible.

9:8-10. This evaluation of old covenant sacrifice stresses two things:

(1) the symbolism of the Holy of Holies as witness to the remoteness and inaccessibility of God;

(2) the importance of sacrifice as the way of expiation of sins. Against the vegetation religions, which insisted on a natural relationship with God through the performance of prescribed ritual, the religion of Israel insisted that God can be known only as God makes the initiative. God can be approached only in the way that has been provided. Israel was a testimony to the grace of God. It showed how God was revealed and opened up an avenue by which men and women can enter God's presence. Compared with vegetation religion the old covenant is the offer of life. Compared to the new covenant it is a reminder of God's remoteness and the tragic difficulty of the human problem.

9:11-14. The priesthood of Christ is now contrasted to the priesthood of the old covenant. The language used is a combination of "time" language and "space" language. The space language contrasts the place of Christ's function with that of the Levitical priesthood. They functioned in the earthly tent which is a copy and shadow of the real. He functions in the **greater and more perfect tent (not made with hands).**

This language, which runs through the entire book, contrasts the perfection, permanence, and fullness of the heavenly priesthood to the imperfection, temporary character, and incompleteness of the earthly priesthood. The career of Jesus represents the intersection of the heavenly with the earthly, the perfect with the imperfect, the eternal with the temporal. It is not a bolt of lightning from beyond, but was prepared in the royal priesthood of Melchizedek (7:1-18). It comes thus as the fulfillment of a process within history, and it is in this way that time and space languages come together in the book.

9:11. The aspect of fulfillment is stressed by the use of the word **appeared,** which might well be rendered "has come," and by the mention of the **good things that have come.** Christ has brought the new age foretold by the prophets. In him the new day breaks in on humanity, the new age of God's gracious work in creation. This line of thought relates to the interpretation of the miracles in the Synoptic gospels, to the understanding of demon exorcism, and to the emphasis on the new age in Paul's letters. What has been true of God from all eternity, what the prophets pointed to as the purpose of the covenant God—this has now broken into the world in the life and ministry of Jesus.

9:12a. The Levitical priesthood approached God through the services of the tabernacle. The great high priest approaches God by entering **once for all into the Holy Place.** Here again time and space vocabularies are interwoven. The death of Christ is an event within earthly history. It took place, as the creeds identify it, "under Pontius Pilate." But it is also an event in eternity. It is the once-for-all entry of the Son, the great high priest, into the presence of God. His death is the true fulfillment of the sacrificial system, for he offered, not the blood of an animal, but his own. His death is the climax of a life offered freely in obedience to the will of God. It is thus a working out in human experience of the inner meaning of tabernacle worship, the offering of one's own life to God. Jesus is not only a man, the son of Mary, but also the Son. Therefore his life is both the offering of God to humanity in his Son and also the act of true human obedience which fulfills and demonstrates the meaning of human existence.

9:12b. Christ's approach to God is by his self-offering as sacrifice, an act in which eternity intersects time. In the cross God provided the sacrifice and showed what sacrifice really means. It is not a human attempt to placate a threatening deity but God's provision of a means by which rebellious and runaway children may be restored to the father's house.

9:12c-14. The result of Christ's sacrifice is an **eternal redemption.** The old sacrifices were effectual. They provided a way of **purification of the flesh.** But the sacrifice of Christ is more effectual. It not only cleanses the body but grants release

to **conscience** so that it may be dedicated to the service of God.
The paradoxical character of the self-offering of Christ is stated
in the words **through the eternal Spirit offered himself.** His life
is God's entry into human affairs. It is also Jesus' offering of
himself **without blemish to God**—a human achievement, the
outcome of a disciplined and dedicated human career.

We find it difficult to hold the two elements together. Either
all is of God or human work is everything. Here the two are in
closest relationship. The self-offering of Christ is a magnificent
human achievement; it is accomplished "through the eternal
spirit." The result of his work is a new era in human life. Those
who live in Christ are already taking part in the messianic age.
They experience the powers of the age to come. They live in the
spirit. United with Christ in his self-offering the Christian
shares in true worship, which is the dedication of oneself to
God's service in union with Jesus Christ.

9:15-22. *The Meaning of Christ's Death.* Because of his
self-offering Christ has become the **mediator of a new covenant.**
Moses served as mediator of the old covenant. This was ratified
by animal sacrifices and the sprinkling of blood on the **people,**
the **book** of the covenant, the **tent,** and all the paraphernalia of
worship. Indeed, the author summarizes, under the old
covenant **almost everything is purified with blood, and without
the shedding of blood there is no forgiveness of sins.**

9:15. Through the offering of blood—that is, the life—the old
covenant prefigures the self-giving of Jesus Christ. His **death,** as
the fulfillment of sacrifice, **redeems** people from **transgressions.**
There is shift here from the language of sacrifice to that of the
commercial world. Redemption is the recovery of an article
given in pledge or the purchase of a slave in the slave market.
The ideas are closely related in the Old Testament and used in
equally close connection in the New Testament. As God
purchased Israel out of slavery in Egypt so in Christ God buys
the people from their bondage in sin and death.

Commercial language is accompanied by that of the lawyer,
the language of wills and inheritances. The death of Christ
procures for those called by God the **promised eternal**

inheritance. It is not something that they have earned or accumulated for themselves. It comes to them from a generous benefactor.

9:16-17. The combination of sacrificial, commercial, and legal language leads to another emphasis on the death of Christ. To us the reference to **covenant** and **will** is obscure. We need to be reminded by a footnote that the same Greek word is used to express both ideas. This verbal coincidence provides basis for the argument that the death of Christ was necessary to the establishment of the new covenant. Here, as in some of the Old Testament quotations, the argument seems lacking in persuasiveness. In this case, however, it is like erecting a supporting scaffold around a tower which is quite capable of standing by itself. The self-offering of Christ is the entry of God's will for human salvation into the course of human history. As such it establishes the new covenant.

9:23-28. *Cleansing of the Heavenly Sanctuary.* In the old covenant sacrificial rites were effective in cleansing the tabernacle and the furniture of worship. If this is true of the copy, it is true also of the heavenly pattern. But whereas the blood of calves and goats was sufficient to cleanse the earthly shrine, the heavenly tabernacle requires **better sacrifices.** And this is the significance of Christ's self-offering. He does not minister in the earthly shrine (cf. 8:4), a **copy of the true one.** He has entered heaven itself and there appears **in the presence of God on our behalf.** Moreover he does not perform this sacrifice **repeatedly,** as the high priest did annually in Israel. He has accomplished it **once for all at the end of the age to put away sin.**

Here again we encounter space language combined with time language. The time language is eschatological—that is, dealing with the end of history. The contrast between the earthly and heavenly shrines, between the temporary and eternal, is joined with the biblical sense of God's purpose moving toward a goal. The goal, or end, appears in the middle of history in Jesus Christ. Thus the author can speak of Christ's coming **at the end of the age.** But Christ still has his people on earth. Therefore there is still movement toward the goal in the life of the church.

Thus the author can speak of Christ's appearing **a second time.** This time he comes **not to deal with sin**—his sacrifice—but to accomplish salvation for **those who are . . . waiting for him.**

Throughout the New Testament we encounter paradoxical language. The kingdom has come in Jesus Christ and yet it is still future. The old age has come to an end with the cross and resurrection of Christ, and the new age has come into being. Yet the old age remains alongside the new. Christians experience the tension between the ages, between the realm of the Spirit and the realm of the flesh. They live in the age to come and yet await the fullness of the inheritance. They exist in the tension between the now and the not yet, between the present reality of the work of God and its future fullness. Attempts are frequently made by theologians to resolve the tensions by stressing only present realization or future completion. But the New Testament writers hold the two together.

9:27-28. These verses offer another comparison between Christ and humanity. Human beings **die once** and then come before God's **judgment.** Christ also has been **offered once**—note the stress on his death as the act of God—and also appears **a second time.** He is not to be judged, however, but to be savior of his people. It is often noted that this is the only explicit reference in the New Testament to a second coming of Christ. Elsewhere the writers speak of his *parousia*—his "coming" or "presence," his manifestation. But it would be a mistake to stress **a second time** in this text. The words appear in the completion of the analogy. The accent falls, not on the word "second," but on the fact that both the death and the reappearance of Christ are distinctively different from those of others.

Christ died, but not as a hapless victim. He offered up his life in freedom, and his death has a sacrificial and redemptive character. When he appears at the judgment, he does not join the long line awaiting assessment. He is Lord of the judgment and savior and deliverer of those who are waiting for him. He voluntarily shared our human experience, and the outcome of his life and death is the transformation of the human situation.

Death once meant only judgment. Those who are Christ's now can look beyond death to the deliverer.

10:1-18. *Contrast of Old and New.* The theological argument of the book comes to its conclusion in this section. Many of the ideas previously presented are repeated, but different aspects are emphasized. The fundamental thesis is by now a familiar one. Worship under the old covenant is a copy of the heavenly pattern, a shadow of the eternal reality. Worship under the new covenant is an entry into the eternal reality.

10:1. The law cannot **make perfect** those who approach God through its institutions. It has only the **shadow of the good things to come.** Its sacrifices are **continually offered year after year,** serving as a reminder of sin but making no permanent purification. The author adds two arguments which are persuasive to those who share his point of view about eternal and temporal realities in worship. They would hardly be persuasive to those within the Jewish community of worship and service. This is one of the considerations which make modern interpreters question the view that the book was written to Jewish Christians who were considering a return to the religion of the old covenant (see Introduction).

10:2-4. A Jew would have no difficulty answering the question in verse 2: **Otherwise would they not have ceased to be offered?** His reply would be that the sacrifices continued because men and women continued to sin. Therefore they were in constant need of atonement and forgiveness. The Jew would also object to the flat assertion that **it is impossible that the blood of bulls and goats should take away sins.** Anyone aware of the prophets' interpretation of sacrifice would recognize that the blood of sacrificial animals had something to do with expiation of sins. This was not because of powers inherent in the blood, but because God had established the institution of sacrifice to enable sinners to draw near and respond to God's grace by the offering of themselves.

From the standpoint of the author, however, the work of Christ has fulfilled sacrifice. Christ has entered the divine presence. The prophetic institutions recede into the background. The author recognizes their usefulness to remind one of sin and to afford expiation under the old covenant. But they pale before the glory of Christ's accomplishments.

10:5-7. The quotation of Psalm 40:6-8 introduces a new emphasis. The author interprets the psalm as being the words of the Messiah and sees in it Christ's interpretation of his own mission. Christ has not come simply to participate in the worship of the old covenant. He does this, but he does more. He accepts the **body,** the life, that God has **prepared** for him. Through it he accomplishes the will of God, as the **roll of the book** has predicted. The language of the psalm—**sacrifices and offerings thou hast not desired**—is not to be read as a rejection of the sacrificial cultus as such. Instead it is the prophetic condemnation of externalized worship, the understanding of covenant religion as a barter transaction with God. It is not the offering of gifts God desires but the offering of self which the offering symbolizes.

10:8-10. Psalm 40 speaks of one who has grasped the prophetic character of covenant religion. Such a person sees life as committed to God, set aside for the divine will. In the career of Jesus Christ the inner meaning of sacrifice is lived out in dedication to God, and sacrifice is thereby fulfilled. Here is the realization that it is not only the hours on the cross that represent the fulfillment of sacrifice. The entire life of Jesus was a life of commitment and dedication. The cross is the climax, the culmination of a life wholly concentrated on the will of God. Sacrifice is therefore abolished—but not in the sense that it had never been useful or that it represented a misunderstanding. Rather it is abolished in the sense that scaffolding is taken down when the building is completed, or temporary approaches removed when a bridge is finished.

10:11-12. The contrast concludes with reference to the frequency of the offering. The priest of the old covenant attends to his work each day, **offering repeatedly the same sacrifices.** But Christ has made **for all time a single sacrifice for sins.** The work of the priest in the old covenant is ineffectual, for he needs constantly to repeat his offerings. But the work of Christ is perfect and complete. When he had made sacrifice for sins, he took his place **at the right hand of God,** the place of rule, authority, and power.

It could be argued that the ineffectual quality of the old sacrifices is overstated. They did, after all, grant assurance of forgiveness to worshipers. It could also be pointed out that Christ's triumph seems to be lacking something, inasmuch as he awaits the subjugation of **his enemies** (verse 13). Both illustrate the taste for overstatement which is characteristic of the Hebrew tradition.

10:13-14. The reference to subjugation of **enemies** introduces again the duality of eschatological language (see above on 9:23-28). Christ has already won his battle and is exalted to power. Yet the final manifestation of his conquests remains in the future. The decisive battle of the war has been fought and the enemy's back has been broken. But the fighting continues; the enemy continues to resist desperately. Nevertheless the biblical writers are confident that with the death and resurrection of Christ the victory is secure. However fierce the struggle only the mopping-up operations remain. The final outcome cannot be changed. God's verdict is in. Those who are set aside for God in Christ have been **perfected for all time** by the single offering of Christ.

10:15-18. Jeremiah's vision of the new covenant is recalled at the end of the discussion (Jeremiah 31:33-34). The author's point at the conclusion of his argument is also affirmed by the **Holy Spirit** speaking through the prophet. When God establishes the new covenant, religion is made a matter of inwardness, putting God's laws in human **hearts.** But even in the new age of inwardness forgiveness is a necessity and is announced as the climax of the prophetic proclamation. Where forgiveness operates, offering for sin is past. With this the author brings his argument to a conclusion. He now turns to the closing section, composed of exhortations and greetings.

IV. ENCOURAGEMENT: MAINTAIN YOUR FAITH (10:19–12:29)

A. AN EXHORTATION TO HOLD FAST (10:19-39)

The third main part of the letter begins with exhortation. In stately, moving language it proceeds through three stages:

(1) a reminder of what the Christian has received through the work of Christ (10:19-25);

(2) a warning of the dangers of drifting into unbelief (10:26-31);

(3) an invitation to recall past encounters with God as a motivation for endurance (10:32-39).

10:19-25. *Response to Christ's Sacrifice.* The exhortation begins by recalling what Christ has accomplished and what the Christian should do in response. It uses the language of worship, adapting the terminology of the tabernacle to the new world inaugurated by the sacrifice of Christ.

The impulse to worship has a twofold source. First is the **confidence** made possible by Christ's self-giving. Second is the living presence of the **great priest** who presides over God's house. The traditional language of Old Testament worship is given heightened meanings in this paragraph as the author summarizes his theological argument. The **sanctuary** is the true sanctuary, the presence of God. The **blood of Jesus** is his self-offering as a sacrifice for sin. The **new and living way . . . through the curtain** means that every Christian may have access to God. This has been won through the obedience of Christ in offering up **his flesh**—that is, his life. Since the conditions of worship have now been transformed by the work of Christ, three exhortations follow:

(1) **Let us draw near** (10:22). The language is again the language of the tabernacle cultus. To "draw near" is the technical term for approaching God in worship. It is possible to do so in confident **faith** because **hearts** have been **sprinkled** and **bodies washed.** The reference to sprinkling recalls the Old Testament sacrifice in which the blood was sprinkled on the altar. The sacrifice which cleanses the Christian is of course that

of Christ. The washing of bodies may be a reference to the ceremonial ablutions of Jewish religion, in which an external ceremonial cleansing symbolized inner purity. It is at least very likely that a reference to the cleansing of baptism is intended here.

(2) **Let us hold fast the confession of our hope** (10:23). "Confession" is the New Testament technical expression for the praise of God. Readers are urged not only to hold to their creed but also to keep a firm grip on the worship of God, which is the content of confession. The characteristic New Testament emphasis on the close interconnection of divine and human activities is also present here. The ground of our worship is the faithfulness of God. We can hold our confession **without wavering** because underneath and behind us is God's reliability.

(3) **Let us consider how to stir up one another to love and good works** (10:24-25). The experience of worship is a community affair. We do not respond automatically to the full meaning of worship. We need to be stimulated. Even in the apostolic age there were people who were **neglecting to meet together** in worship and needed encouragement. The expectation of a short interval between the crucifixion and the **Day** of the return of the victorious Christ supplies such a stimulus. The enduring value of this hope is its motivation to life in the spirit of Christ.

10:26-31. *A Warning Against Apostasy.* Like the earlier passage on the impossibility of a second repentance (6:4-8) this warning is expressed in strong language. The analogy of the old covenant is the starting point. **Sacrifice** atoned only for sins of ignorance. There was no atonement for sins committed **deliberately.** Apostasy is no less perilous in the new covenant. Death was the lot of one who **violated the law of Moses** (cf. Deuteronomy 17:2-6). Worse than death will be the fate of one **who has spurned the Son of God,** treated the **blood of the covenant** as a common thing, and **outraged the Spirit of grace.** God is indeed gracious. But God remains God and is not to be taken lightly. Divine mercy draws men and women back to

45

God's purpose. It does not license them to do as they will. One who does not respect the grace of God will discover that God judges people and that it is a frightful thing to meet God apart from Jesus Christ.

10:32-39. *The Need for Endurance.* This passage of encouragement also echoes an earlier discussion (6:9-12). The author seeks to stir his readers from their complacency by reminding them of more heroic times in their own history. They once endured **sufferings . . . abuse . . . affliction.** They helped others in such trials. They showed mercy to **prisoners,** and **accepted** the loss of their **property.** They were able to do so because they were convinced that in faith they had a **better possession**—one that endured. Since that time their **confidence** in God has been neglected. The author warns them not to **throw** it **away,** for it promises a **great reward.** They have real need of staying power so that they may **do the will of God** and receive the promised inheritance.

The exhortation concludes with a quotation from the Septuagint translation of Habakkuk 2:3*d*-4—preceded by a phrase appearing in Isaiah 26:20—in which the order is transposed so that it appears to be the **righteous one** who **shrinks back.** The author expresses assurance that he and his readers will not be such drop-outs. They will maintain faith and **keep their souls.**

B. The Triumphs of Faith (11:1-40)

The exhortation of chapter 10 climaxes in the appeal for steadfeast and loyal faith. The power and wonder of faith is now exalted in a rapturous hymn. It has six parts or movements:

(1) a definition of faith with a brief summary of its past and present benefits (verses 1-3);

(2) a review of what faith accomplished from Abel to Abraham and Sarah (verses 4-12);

(3) a summary of the pilgrim character of faith (verses 13-16);

(4) a recalling of what faith accomplished from Abraham to the settlement in the Promised Land (verses 17-31);

(5) a summary of what people have been able to accomplish through faith (verses 32-38);

(6) a transition concerning the communion of believers (verses 39-40).

11:1-3. *A Definition of Faith.* The description of faith in verse 1 shows the same characteristics of language noted earlier. There is a combination of space and time language. Faith is seen in both dimensions. **Assurance** is used in ancient commercial documents in the sense of "title deed." Faith as title deed of good things to come combines the elements of hope, confidence, and trust. This parallels Paul's understanding of the presence of the spirit as "earnest money" guaranteeing the inheritance, or as "first fruits" assuring the harvest. By faith the believer has title to good things to come. One is convinced that the divine realm is indeed real.

11:2-3. In the past faith brought **divine approval** to those who trusted God. In the present it enables us to understand that the things we see and touch are actually dependent on what is invisible to us. Faith is the encounter with God in which a taste of God's goodness enables us to trust in God—even without the evidence necessary to convince a skeptic. By faith we can understand life as God's gift and see the world as God's creation.

11:4-16. *Early Witnesses to Faith.* The Old Testament patriarchs were asked to trust God without much supporting evidence. By the courage and confidence of their faith they still speak encouragement to us. **Abel** saw that the deepest meaning of **sacrifice** is trust in God. The common interpretation of Genesis 5:24 as meaning that **Enoch** did **not see death** appears in the Septuagint translation **taken up. Pleased God,** the Septuagint translation of "walked with God," testifies to Enoch's faith.

Noah endured the mocking of his contemporaries to obey God's commandment. **Abraham** went out into a **foreign land** at God's command. He gave up the securities of family, home, and religion and risked everything at the word of one he had not previously encountered. **Sarah,** in a situation which was humanly speaking impossible, trusted in God's faithfulness.

11:13-16. All these people died without seeing the fulfillment of **what was promised.** Thus it might seem that their faith was in vain. But they looked forward in hope to God's promise, rejecting the temptation to turn back. Their lives show that they were concentrating on a **better country, that is, a heavenly one.** Therefore God is **not ashamed** to be identified with them and **has prepared for them a city.** The vision of the city as prosperous and peaceful, secure against its enemies, has been a favorite image of religious thinkers in many traditions.

11:17-31. *More Witnesses to Faith.* The succession of heroes of faith continues. It resumes with **Abraham** and moves forward in time to the exodus and settlement in Cannaan. Abraham showed the quality of his faith when God asked for the sacrifice of his son. **Isaac** was the heir through whom the **promises** were to be fulfilled. Yet Abraham obeyed in the belief that God would still find some way to keep his word. The other patriarchs are listed as examples of faith. Then **Moses** is considered. He found life through the faith of **his parents,** who trusted God and defied the **edict** of Pharaoh. By faith he chose to share the fate of his countrymen and led them out of **Egypt** and through the **Red Sea.** By faith **Jericho** was conquered, and **Rahab** was spared the fate of her fellow citizens.

11:32-38. *Summary of Faith's Accomplishments.* The rhetorical question **And what more shall I say?** suggests that the story could be continued indefinitely. But the catalog of heroes comes to an end, and another method of summation is employed. Instead of listing heroes of faith up to the time of the gospel, the author lists instead the achievements of believers— temptations overcome, persecutions endured, life won from the jaws of death. It is an eloquent and impressive account of steadfast faith in the presence of disaster. It is the story of people whose hope was fixed on the promise of God and could not be diverted by persuasion or threats—those **of whom the world was not worthy.**

11:39-40. *The Communion of Believers.* Verse 39 seems a disappointing ending to so heroic an account. Then we realize what use the author is making of his catalog. However great their achievement, these giants of faith **did not receive what was promised**—not because God's word failed, but because God willed that believers of all times should share in the joy and triumph of the new age inaugurated by Christ. If faith could win such victories under such difficult conditions in the old covenant, how much more will faith accomplish in the new age! Now one lives in the sure knowledge of God's favor in Jesus Christ, possesses the gifts of the Spirit, and tastes the powers of the age to come.

The preacher skillfully conceals a rebuke beneath an inspirational account of past heroes. He seeks to move his readers to ask themselves, "If they did so much with so little, what will be expected of us who live in the day of fulfillment?" The faithful of other generations do not reach their destiny alone. It is in fellowship with contemporary believers that they are **made perfect.**

C. Therefore Take Courage! (12:1-29)

12:1-2. *The Race of Life.* The third stage brings the exhortation to a close. The heroes of the past have been reviewed. They stand by, watching anxiously to see how God's people fare. Since we have such a distinguished **cloud of witnesses,** let us put aside our anxieties and cares. Let us put off the sin that besets us, and **let us run with perseverance.** The **race** is a long run, where speed may be of less importance than endurance.

If the witnesses do not stimulate us to make an effort, there remains one motivation—the example of **Jesus.** He is **the pioneer and perfecter of our faith,** who needed the utmost courage and stamina for his ministry. He has broken the trail for us. He also enables us to follow his path. His mission in life required great personal effort. He needed motivation, even as we do. His motivation was the joy of doing God's will. He

endured the cross, despising the shame. Thus he won the victory, and now shares the **throne** of the universe.

12:3-11. *Consideration of the Life of Christ.* Whatever the readers have undergone, they cannot seriously maintain that their **struggle against sin** has brought them **to the point of shedding . . . blood.** Christ's obedience was unto death. He has not promised to let his disciples off more easily. Moreover, their trials are sent, not to discourage, but to **discipline.** This is illustrated by a quotation from Proverbs 3:11-12. It is a sign that **God is treating** us **as sons.** The father who does not discipline his sons does not thereby demonstrate his love but treats them as **illegitimate children,** in whom he has no pride.

Two other analogies occur to the author:

(1) We have endured the discipline of **earthly fathers.** How much more should we endure that of the **Father** of all the living!

(2) Earthly fathers discipline us only during our childhood and may be erratic and arbitrary about it. God **disciplines us for our good, that we may share his holiness.** The final remark of the section reminds that all discipline is hard and **painful.** It can be appreciated only in its outcome, **the peaceful fruit of righteousness.**

12:12-17. *An Admonition to Respond.* The exhortation becomes specific. The problem of the readers is evidently not overwhelming difficulties but lack of resolution. They have simply not planned intelligently or worked with energy. **Peace** and **holiness** will not drop on them like snow from heaven. They must **strive** for them. The center of the problem in verse 15 has been intimated in earlier exhortations (2:1; 3:6; 5:11-14). They do not appropriate the **grace of God.** They apparently expect God to do everything. They fail to understand that God has done the work and now awaits the response of the believer. Those who like to hear about God's goodness and never exert themselves become a **root of bitterness** (Deuteronomy 29:18). They are a source of contention which then infects an entire community with bickering and jealousy.

The outcome of this is shown in the experience of **Esau,** who in his impatient appetite **sold his birthright for a single meal.**

When he later came to his senses and claimed the **blessing,** it was too late. Even his **tears** were of no avail—another somber warning about the problem of a second repentance (cf. 6:4-8; 10:26).

12:18-29. *The New Accessibility of God's Holiness.* The awful and frightening events which accompanied the giving of the old covenant are contrasted to the graciousness and tenderness of God's love in Christ. Sinai is portrayed in exaggerated language: **fire . . . darkness . . . gloom . . . tempest . . . sound of a trumpet . . . a voice** so terrifying that those who heard it were appalled. But the same God who is disclosed as dread mystery at Sinai now invites our approach to a **heavenly Jerusalem**—to **angels** in festive array, to an **assembly** of the elect, to God the **judge,** and to **Jesus, the mediator of the new covenant.**

An examination of the details shows how carefully this passage has been constructed to contrast two dramatic scenes of revelation. Both are awesome, but are quite different in total impression. The approach to Sinai suggests an experience so intense as to be emotionally disintegrating. The approach to heaven itself could be even more awesome. But the author manages to make it sound hospitable, the kind of environment in which humans can feel at home even though it is unsettling in its overpowering graciousness.

12:25-29. This contrast gives the setting for listening to the gospel. When God spoke **on earth,** God's warning was awesome. No one who refused could escape. But now in Christ, God has spoken **from heaven. How much less shall we escape** if we reject him! At Sinai **his voice . . . shook the earth.** The voice from heaven **will shake not only the earth but also the heaven** (Haggai 2:6). When this happens, all that is changeable will be removed so that **what cannot be shaken may remain.** The exhortation ends on a positive note, not frightening or threatening. Christians can be grateful for this reason—**we have received a kingdom that cannot be shaken.** And we can **offer to God acceptable worship, with reverence and awe.**

This closing section well illustrates the remarkable capacity of the author to combine two elements of the Christian religion in an impressive synthesis. Few writers excel him in presenting the awful majesty and holiness of God. Not many succeed as well in presenting the approachability and graciousness of God in Christ. Fewer still keep the two together in such close connection in their teaching.

V. EPILOGUE: EXHORTATIONS, BENEDICTION, GREETINGS (13:1-25)

This closing chapter may be an addition to the original work (see Introduction). It has five sections:
  (1) exhortations concerning the conduct of Christians (verses 1-6);
  (2) urgings for respect toward leaders (verses 7-17);
  (3) an appeal for intercessory prayer (verses 18-19);
  (4) benediction (verses 20-21);
  (5) greetings (verses 22-25).

13:1-6. *Exhortations on Conduct.* The first section urges **brotherly love** and **hospitality,** compassion for prisoners and sufferers, respect for the purity of **marriage,** and freedom from covetousness. The exhortation to hospitality recalls the experience of Abraham (Genesis 18:1-8; 19:1-3). The reference to being **in the body** would be construed as a reference to the church as body of Christ if it occurred in a Pauline letter. Here it is probably no more than a reminder that the readers too live on the physical level. Therefore they should be sympathetic to those who suffer. God's faithfulness and care is urged as the ground for avoiding covetousness.

13:7-17. *Respect for Leaders.* This section suggests that there have been tensions between the leaders and the people, perhaps over questions of doctrine and ascetic practices. That Jesus Christ is included in the circle of leaders is somewhat surprising but quite appropriate. It recalls that Christ is also one of us. He has shared our human experience, which thereby makes him accessible to us as an example. It also reminds the leaders that they are to be conformed to Christ. He won his leadership of God's people by submission to the cross. There is no other pattern for his followers.

13:9-14. The **strange teachings** referred to here are difficult to identify. The reference to **foods** suggests that it involved a form of asceticism or abstention from certain foods. The teaching, whatever it was, is rejected for two reasons:

(1) The proper nourishment of man is the **grace** of God. Therefore distinction of foods has no significant place in the religion of the gospel.

(2) **We have an altar,** the eternal one in heaven, from which the priests **have no right to eat.** Even in the old covenant the flesh of the animal offered in the sin offering was not used in a sacrificial meal but was **burned outside the camp** (Leviticus 16:27). In the new covenant **Jesus . . . suffered outside the gate.** The argument seems to be that foods cannot be brought into the center of Christian worship. That is, they have no relation to forgiveness and life with God. Even in the old covenant food was separated from the ritual of atonement. In the new the atoning sacrifice itself takes place, not in the sanctuary, but on a hill outside the city.

The Christian therefore leaves the sanctuary with its ritual requirements and goes with the Lord **outside the camp,** sharing his humiliation. **Here we have no lasting city,** no permanent community with its rules and regulations. Christians are a pilgrim community on the way, seeking a settled life to come.

13:15-16. The worship that we offer God is therefore not the worship of a legally regulated ritual. It is the **sacrifice of praise . . . , the fruit of lips that acknowledge his name.** The word "name" here, as elsewhere in the Bible, is a shorthand expression for all the deeds of God by which God is disclosed to human beings. To **acknowledge his name** is therefore more than giving a passing gesture of recognition. It is to relate oneself seriously to God's self-disclosure, to accept Jesus Christ as God's definitive word. This worship is not limited to what we call liturgical acts. It is liturgy in the older sense, the worship and praise of God which includes acts of mercy, kindness, love, and service. **Such sacrifices are pleasing to God.**

13:17. Readers are reminded of their obligations to their leaders. The author suggests with almost humorous irony that leaders be permitted to work out their responsibilities **joyfully, and not sadly.** After all, sadness does not benefit the congregation.

13:18-19. *An Appeal for Intercessory Prayer.* The references to a **clear conscience** and to acting **honorably in all things** may imply that the author is in prison, in circumstances which might be embarrassing to his readers. His wish to be **restored** to them may be read as supporting this suggestion. Other explanations are also possible, however.

13:20-21. *Benediction.* This beautiful benediction and doxology contains one of the few references to the resurrection in the book. It also sums up ideas expressed at greater length earlier—the sacrifice of Christ, the establishment of a new covenant, and the life of the Christian as both the work of God and a matter of his own exertions.

13:22-24. *Greetings.* The closing lines appeal for receptivity. They offer an item of news about a co-worker and express the author's hope to visit his readers. The book concludes with greetings.

13:23. Though no doubt there were a number of early Christians bearing the same name, **our brother Timothy** is generally assumed to refer to the well-known associate of Paul (cf. II Corinthians 1:1; Colossians 1:1; I Thessalonians 3:2; Philemon 1). This reference may have been largely responsible for the attribution of the book to Paul. Some suspect that it was added to the work specifically to give such an impression. On the other hand Timothy was apparently quite young when he joined Paul (cf. Philemon 2:22; I Timothy 4:12). Thus he may have continued to be an active leader in the church throughout the remainder of the first century. There is no reason to doubt that he could have been known both to the author of this book and to the readers he addressed (see Introduction).

13:24-25. The author concludes with **greetings** to both **leaders** and **saints** (church members) and his wish that the favor of God may be with them. **Those who come from Italy** is literally "they from [or "of"] Italy." This ambiguous phrase might mean Italians either at home or abroad. Therefore it offers no clue as to the whereabouts of the author and his companions (see Introduction).

THE LETTER OF JAMES

Richard L. Scheef, Jr.

INTRODUCTION

Nature and Purpose

To benefit from the letter of James, the reader must first
understand the kind of book that is being read. It would be a
mistake to look into James for profound theology. The letter is
no such theological treatise. It is rather a collection of moral
exhortations (see below on 1:1). The author's subject is the
practice of the Christian life. To this end he compiles a collection
of teachings to give specific directions to Christians—things
they should do or not do, attitudes they should adopt, and others
they should reject. The mood of the letter is imperative, its tone
hortatory, and its purpose practical.

In collecting such teachings as these the author was following
a practice already established by other early Christian writers.
For example, Paul added a collection of practical instructions to
his letter to the Romans (chapters 12–15; cf. the lists of
household duties in Ephesians 5:21–6:9; Colossians 3:18–4:1;
and I Peter 2:18–3:7). A comparison of the collections of ethical
instructions within the New Testament reveals many similarities of subject matter, style, and mood. This has led many
scholars to conclude that the churches of New Testament times
borrowed previously existing traditions of moral instruction

from Jewish and Greek philosophical or religious sources and incorporated them in the Christian teaching.

It is important to notice how each New Testament author relates his moral teaching to the Christian gospel, which has its center in the person of Jesus Christ. One, for example, exhorts his readers to follow the example of Christ in patience and suffering (I Peter 2:21-24; 4:1). Another calls readers to be "imitators of God" and to "walk in love, as Christ loved us and gave himself for us" (Ephesians 5:1-2). In each case the moral exhortation is based upon some aspect of the life and work of Jesus Christ.

The author of James does not state his christological foundation for ethical teaching. Rather he assumes it and proceeds into the moral teaching itself. This has led some students to regard James as inferior to other books in the New Testament canon. They assign to it a "subcanonical" status. The well-known example of this attitude is Martin Luther's designation of James as an "epistle of straw" because it did not witness to Christ in the Pauline manner.

In this light, James *is* inferior to the letters of Paul. On the other hand, if one simply lets the author speak his own mind in his own way and to his own purpose, then the book can be appreciated for what it really is. What does a Christian *do* about faith (2:14-26)? What should be the Christian's attitude toward the rich and the poor in the congregation (2:1-7), or the correct thought as a journey is contemplated (4:13-15)? These are the kinds of questions helpfully answered in the letter.

If James is primarily a collection of practical instructions, is it really a letter in the usual sense of that term? Outside the opening salutation there is little in the book to indicate that it was intended as a personal communication. Instead the author has merely collected and edited traditional materials for circulation among churches throughout the world (see below on 1:1).

Authorship

The author of the letter identifies himself in 1:1 as "James, a servant of God and of the Lord Jesus Christ." He tells us little else about himself except that he is a teacher (3:1). He sends no greetings to his readers at the end of the letter, and there is no formal closing which would give any clue about either the writer or the recipients of the letter. Thus we have only the name James to tell us who wrote the letter. But who is James?

The traditional view is that the author is James the Lord's brother, the leader of the Jerusalem church. He was in contact with Paul (cf. Galatians 1:19; 2:9, 12, and Acts 15:13). He could have written to correct a false view of Paul's teaching on faith and works (cf. 2:14-26). Many scholars, however, find reasons for questioning this tradition.

First, the letter does not seem to have been known in early Christian churches until the time of Origen at the close of the second century. A document composed by a person as prominent as James of Jerusalem would certainly have been widely circulated and known before that time.

Second, there is nothing in the letter itself to indicate a close relationship between the author and Jesus. Though some passages allude to the teachings of Jesus, the author uses Hellenistic and Jewish traditions as his primary sources. A person in the position of James of Jerusalem would probably not compile such traditions. Rather he would write on his own authority and on the basis of the Lord's teachings.

Last, the author uses excellent Greek. Such facility would be unlikely in an Aramaic-speaking Jew of Jerusalem.

None of these arguments is conclusive as evidence against the traditional view. But their cumulative effect makes it hard to believe that James of Jerusalem is the author. It seems more probable that someone compiled a set of Christian teachings and sent them out to the churches of the world under the name of the Lord's brother.

The name the author chose had meaning for his readers in another way. "James" is the English translation of the Hebrew and Greek "Jacob," which immediately suggests the father of the twelve tribes of Israel. The author or editor probably selected this name to suggest that the church as the new Israel has a new patriarchal authority in the person of James ("Jacob") of Jerusalem (see below on 1:1).

The Readers

James is addressed to Christians scattered throughout the world rather than to the members of a particular local congregation (see below on 1:1). Though the opening verse suggests that both author and addressees were Jewish Christians, the teachings of the letter are not exclusively Jewish. Nor are they addressed to Jews alone. These are moral teachings applicable to Jews and Gentiles alike. The intended recipients of the letter, therefore, could be Christians anywhere who need moral instruction in the specific duties of practical Christianity.

Thus James is written for all Christians who claim to believe but do not act (2:14-26), who let their partiality go unchecked (2:1-7), who blame God for their temptations (1:13), who fail to control their tongues (3:2ff.), who let strife run wild (4:1ff.), etc. All such attitudes and actions make a mockery of true religion. Against this kind of sham the author urges his readers to embrace pure religion in which belief and conduct, words and deeds form a unified and beneficial whole.

Date of Composition

If James is a collection of traditions and moralistic instructions, the formation of these traditions could have taken place quite early. A recent study claims that what is reflected in James is a simple and undeveloped piety which might have been employed in the Galilean ministry of Jesus.

The teachings of James do in some respects echo those of Jesus. But the variety of the collection shows that the author gathered his material from no single source. Probably he collected some Jewish, some Greek, and some Christian teachings and put them all together in his letter. Some of these traditions might even be older than the time of Jesus—for example, those which seem to parallel the Old Testament, especially Proverbs. On the other hand, some might have originated later than the missionary work of Paul—for example, the passage on faith and works in 2:14-26.

The question remains: When was the collection made and put into its present form? If we assume that the letter was written to combat a corrupted and misinterpreted form of Paul's teaching, it must be dated sometime after Paul's major work—that is, past the middle of the first century. Further, on the supposition that Paul's teaching was not too widespread until after his letters were collected about A.D. 95, the final composition of James must then be dated about 100-125.

Status in the New Testament

As already noted some theologians and scholars like Luther have considered James inferior among the documents of the New Testament. This opinion has some foundation in the early history of the book among New Testament writings. The first Christian writer to accept it as canonical was Origen at the close of the second century. He probably brought it with him from Caesarea to Alexandria. Origen is responsible for its acceptance in that city as a work of James the Lord's brother.

Meanwhile, in the churches of the west, James remained relatively unknown. Jerome included it in his translation of the Bible, the Vulgate, around A.D. 382. This probably led to its eventual acceptance as a canonical book in the west. Following Jerome, Augustine (around A.D. 354-430) also accepted it as canonical. It was accepted as such in the councils of Hippo in 393 and Carthage in 397 and 419.

Thus James was viewed with some doubts from the beginning. Even though it was eventually accepted as canonical, it has always had a hard time winning its way to an authentic status among the letters of the New Testament. Nevertheless, because of its down-to-earth teaching and quotable maxims, the letter enjoys wide popular appeal.

I. SALUTATION (1:1)

Following the customary form for letters in his day, the author names himself, designates the addressees, and greets them.

James is the English translation of the Greek and Hebrew name "Jacob," the father of the twelve sons representing the tribes of Israel (see Introduction). The name itself would immediately suggest to the original readers that the author is following an Old Testament model of some kind. In Genesis 49 there is a collection of blessings pronounced by the aged Jacob upon each of his twelve sons. Though the letter has little more than a general resemblance to these blessings, the similarity hints at intentional connection. Perhaps the author wants to suggest that, just as Jacob of old addressed himself to his twelve sons representing the tribes of Israel, so now a "Christian patriarch" of the same name writes to the church as the new Israel.

Twelve tribes would be clearly understood by the original readers as an allusion to the whole nation of Israel. The **Dispersion** was understood to designate the Jews who were scattered in various parts of the world outside their homeland of Palestine. To Christians, however, **the twelve tribes in the Dispersion** would clearly mean that the letter is addressed to the church as the new Israel and to all the followers of Christ scattered throughout the world. For this reason the letter has sometimes been classified with others like I and II Peter and Jude as general, or catholic, epistles.

Outside the opening verse there is little in this "letter" which looks like a personal communication. The author does not seem to know his readers personally. He does not speak of the problems or concerns of Christians in a particular place, as Paul addresses himself in a personal way to his fellow Christians of Corinth, Thessalonica, or Philippi. Rather the collection of teachings reflects generally accepted moral principles which might be applied in any church.

II. GENERAL EXHORTATIONS (1:2-18)

The first major section consists of a collection of miscellaneous exhortations. The subjects of the various teachings gathered here seem to be unrelated to each other and are loosely organized. The author moves abruptly from one subject to another without apparent transition. Yet there are "tag words" which serve as connecting links between some of the varied subjects—for example, **steadfastness** in verses 3-4, **lacking** and **lacks** in verses 4-5, **ask** in verses 5-6. This suggests that the collection was put together in oral form. The tag words aided memory and recitation.

1:2-4. *Through Trials to Full Life.* The church in the Dispersion was made up of people who found themselves in an alien and sometimes hostile world. That they endured **trials** or persecution which tested their faithfulness is evident throughout the New Testament. Rather than let these adversities defeat them, the readers of this letter are to rejoice because such trials provide the testing which strengthens faith and leads to full and meaningful life. Cf. the similar description in Romans 5:3-5, where Paul traces the movement from suffering to hope; also I Peter 1:6-7, where the trials of Christians are likened to the refiner's fire.

Faith in verse 3, in contrast to its meaning in 2:14-26, means not mere belief but faithfulness. What is being tested is not a body of doctrine but fidelity in action. Such a testing **produces** (literally "works out") **steadfastness,** or endurance, as Paul calls it in Romans 5:3. Such steadfastness has its **full effect** in the long-range result that the Christian **may be perfect and complete, lacking in nothing.** These last terms define each other. **Perfect** denotes, not absolute sinlessness, but wholeness—the kind of life which is filled with meaningful purpose and which leaves nothing to be desired. Because their life has this meaning and goal, Christians can and should **count it all joy** when confronted with various trials.

1:5-8. *Pray in Faith.* The main point of the next teaching is that God gives freely in answer to prayers made in faith. **Wisdom,** essential to the full Christian life, is a gift of God and will be discussed more fully in 3:13-18. Anyone who lacks this virtue should **ask God who gives to all men generously.** God gives **without reproaching**—that is, without condescension which spoils the gift. **Faith** is the opposite of doubt. It is firm trust in God like that of Abraham, who did not waver in unbelief (cf. Romans 4:18-21; also the teaching of Jesus on faith and effective prayer in Matthew 21:21-22 and Luke 17:6). Like a wind-driven wave, the person who doubts is **unstable in all his ways.** His **double-minded** wavering runs throughout all his attitudes and actions. It destroys the relationship of full trust in God. The person who lacks faith is cut off from God and will not **receive anything from the Lord.**

1:9-11. *Riches Pass Away.* Although these verses contrast lowliness and riches, the main thrust is against riches, as in 2:5-9 and 5:1-6. The **lowly brother** may **boast** or rejoice **in his exaltation** because he is rich in faith and an heir of God's kingdom (cf. 2:5; Matthew 6:19-21; Luke 6:20). On the other hand, the **rich** person's riches will pass away **like the flower of the grass** (cf. Isaiah 40:6-7).

1:12-15. *Blessed Trials and Ruinous Temptations.* Verse 12 picks up the theme of **trial** from verses 2-4. It adds a new dimension to the happiness of the one who endures: **He will receive the crown of life** guaranteed to those who love God.

1:13-15. In Greek the same word means both "trial" and "temptation." In verse 13 there is a switch to the verbal form of the second meaning—to "lure" or "entice." Such enticements do not come from God. Since God is only good and is beyond temptation, **he himself tempts no one.** A person cannot blame God for temptations since they arise from **his own desire** or lust. Illicit desires, when allowed to run their course, give rise to **sin.** In this letter sin means the failure to do right or the neglect of good deeds (cf. 2:9; 4:17). The disastrous consequence of sin is that, like a malignant growth, it brings **death** (cf. Romans 5:12-21; 6:20-23; 7:8-11).

1:16-18. *All Good Gifts Come from God.* To say, "I am tempted by God" (verse 13), is to deceive oneself (verse 16). On the contrary, God gives only good and perfect gifts. God is **the Father of lights,** who is light and who creates light and the heavenly bodies (cf. Genesis 1:3; Psalm 136:7-9). With God **there is no variation or shadow due to change.** Though the exact meaning of this last phrase is not clear, the purpose is probably to contrast the unchanging light of God with that of heavenly bodies which do change.

1:18. Compare the use of **word** here with the meanings in the following passage, verses 21-23. The **word of truth** here refers to God's creative power by which we were made **first fruits** of all created things and beings. In Christian usage, however, it may mean God's creative power which continues to regenerate us through the gospel, that we might be the first fruits of the new age in Christ (cf. Romans 8:19-23; I Corinthians 15:20; Revelation 14:4).

III. THE WAY TO PURE RELIGION (1:19-27)

Hear and do. These are the ingredients of true piety. The way to pure religion is to receive the word and to apply it in concrete deeds of charity.

1:19-21. *Receive the Saving Word.* The imperative **know this** engages the reader's attention. It marks the beginning of a new section dealing with the author's practical concept of true religion. This begins with receptivity: **Be quick to hear** not only the **word** but also whatever is said. The ability of Christians to help one another often begins with the willingness to listen to each other. The attentive listener will be **slow to speak.**

1:20. The religious person will be **slow to anger,** for anger does not bear the fruit of true piety. **The righteousness of God** is a profound and dynamic concept in Paul's thought (cf. Romans 1:16-17; 3:21). Here it has a practical meaning—namely the good deeds which God requires.

1:21. The path to true religion is obstructed by **filthiness** and **wickedness.** The Christian must put aside these evils and receive the **implanted word** of the gospel, which is able to save the soul. True religion has an inner core which is the source of piety and action. To the author this center is the **implanted word,** which is Christian teaching, **the law of liberty** (verse 25), and **the royal law** (2:8).

1:22-25. *Doing the Word.* True religion begins by receiving the word. But hearing alone would be an empty and meaningless thing. The word must lead to deeds (verse 22). The author's insistence on good deeds anticipates his teaching that faith without works is dead (2:14-26).

1:23-24. A person who hears but does not do the word is like one who casually looks at them in a **mirror** and then turns away without further thought. Nothing happens to change them or their ways.

1:25. But one who looks into the **perfect law** and does not forget but perseveres and acts—this person **shall be blessed in his doing.** The law of God was already thought of as the perfect law in Old Testament times. To the author of James the perfect law—like the implanted word of verse 21 and the royal law of 2:8—is the law of God as understood in the Old Testament and as interpreted by Jesus in the gospels. By calling it the **law of liberty** he reflects the then current Jewish teaching that obedience to the law is true freedom.

1:26-27. *Pure Religion.* It has already been said that the religious person is "slow to speak" (verse 19). More than that, he must **bridle his tongue.** The person who **thinks he is religious** and does not control his tongue deceives himself. Such religion is merely an empty form.

1:27. Ritual purity and spotlessness was universally required in all ancient religions. It was insisted on by pious Jews and Pharisees in New Testament times (cf. Mark 7:3-4). Only the **pure and undefiled** is acceptable to God. Such pure religion is first defined as **to visit orphans and widows**—that is, to work the works of justice and charity. Secondly, such religion is **to keep oneself unstained from the world** by avoiding involvement in the wickedness which inevitably surrounds Christians scattered abroad.

IV. Partiality Is Sin (2:1-13)

Chapter 2 is less miscellaneous than chapter 1. It is organized around two major themes: partiality (verses 1-13) and faith and works (verses 14-26). Moreover, the style of chapter 2 differs from that of chapter 1. Instead of stringing together various exhortations by means of tag words, as in chapter 1, the author now employs the style of the diatribe. This was a technique or oral discourse used by Greek Stoic and Cynic philosophers in which the speaker acted as if he were carrying on a dialogue with an imaginary person. One characteristic of this style which appears frequently in chapter 2 is the use of rhetorical questions—for example, verses 4, 5, 15-16, and 20.

2:1-7. *No Partiality in Church.* Partiality, meaning regard for outward appearance, is incompatible with Christian faith (verse 1). God does not look on outward appearance. Jesus obviously did not cater to the rich or powerful, but humbled himself and associated with ordinary people. The one who is **the Lord of glory,** who reflected the power and presence of God, humbled himself and appeared in the form of a servant.

2:2-4. Nor should partiality ever find its way into the Christian **assembly** (literally "synagogue," but verse 1 makes clear that a Christian congregation is meant). The example of partiality is obvious. Do not favor the rich and well-dressed by offering them a seat, while at the same time providing no seat at all for the poor or letting them sit on the floor. The persons who make such **distinctions** set themselves up as **judges** with ulterior motives.

2:5-7. Such distinctions are contrary to the fact that God has **chosen those who are poor in the world** to receive blessings (cf. 1:9-11). To favor the rich would dishonor the **poor man,** the very one whom God would exalt. In addition, there is little to be gained by favoring the rich. They are the very ones who **oppress** Christians and **drag** them **into court.** The author seems to have in mind rich outsiders who are unsympathetic to Christians and who also **blaspheme** or despise the very **name** of God by which God's people are called.

2:8-13. *Partiality Is Against God's Law.* The **royal law,** like the "perfect law" in 1:25, refers to the whole law of God revealed in the Old Testament and interpreted by Jesus and in Christian tradition. The law is summed up in the commandment to **love**

your neighbor. The Christian will do well to comply with it—even with respect to the rich.

2:9-11. On the other hand, partiality is a violation of another part of the law (cf. Leviticus 19:15). To break any part of the law is to **commit sin.** Whoever breaks one part of the law is **guilty of all of it.**

2:12-13. The Christian is to obey the whole law of God in all its parts. Only full obedience achieves freedom and makes it a **law of liberty** (cf. 1:25). The teaching of Jesus clearly shows that mercy will not be given to the person who shows **no mercy** (Matthew 18:23-35). Yet **mercy triumphs over judgment** in the sense that the one who shows mercy will receive it (Matthew 5:7).

V. FAITH PRODUCES WORKS (2:14-26)

This passage is probably the most famous of all in James. **Faith apart from works is dead** (verse 26) is an oft-quoted maxim. It has wide popular appeal because it makes good common sense. The author is obviously correcting a false notion about faith. Some people apparently thought that faith was mere belief in certain doctrines like the unity of God. Such belief is not faith, for **even the demons** can **believe** that much! (verse 19). True faith, rather, is the kind of belief which produces good works.

Where did such false ideas of faith arise? Our lack of complete knowledge of the circumstances in which the letter was composed prevents us from answering this question with certainty. Yet the fact that "faith alone" was a basic doctrine of Paul suggests that 2:14-26 was directed against a distorted form of Paul's teaching. The fact that Abraham, one of Paul's favorite Old Testament characters, is used to illustrate the point gives added weight to this supposition.

Although the author differs with Paul on the meaning of faith and its relationship to works, the apparent conflicts can be reconciled. To Paul, faith is the deep personal relationship of trust in Christ in which the believer receives God's grace. Faith is a living relationship in which the believer is re-created and empowered to live the Christian life as described by Paul in Romans 5–8. Surely the notion that faith is mere belief which excuses a person from action and responsibility is far from Paul's understanding.

The author tackles this heresy by affirming the necessary relationship between faith and works. Belief becomes faith only when it produces action. To be sure, he lacks Paul's profundity. Unlike Paul, he does not think of faith as a living relationship between the believer and Christ. Rather, to him faith is sincere belief which is accompanied and validated by good works.

2:14-17. *Faith Without Works Is Dead.* Consistency of belief and action constitutes true faith. On the contrary, belief without action is of no profit and cannot save a person. An obvious example in verses 15-16 makes the point. Mere words cannot clothe or fill a person in need. Without the articles of clothing and food such words are hollow sounds. Similarly, belief alone **is dead**—that is, such supposed "faith" is not faith at all.

2:18-19. *The Unity of Faith and Works.* Faith and works are two sides of the same reality. Faith is the inner side of action; works are the outward expression of faith. Even **demons** can believe in the unity of God—and **shudder** in their fear. But obviously such belief which does not result in good works is vain.

2:20-26. *Abraham's Works and Faith.* The point of the interrelationship between faith and works is now illustrated. The rhetorical question in verse 20 is hurled at an imaginary **shallow man,** who is foolish to twist Paul's teaching into such an obvious error.

2:21-24. To understand the point here, cf. the thought in Romans 4. Paul bases his doctrine of "faith alone" on Abraham's complete trust in God (Genesis 15:1-6). The stress here is on the deeds of Abraham, specifically the sacrifice of Isaac (cf. Genesis 22:1-19). The point is that Abraham's faith was not mere belief. His **faith was active along with his works,** and it **was completed by works.** It is this kind of faith, evinced and completed by good deeds, which counts as **righteousness.** In Romans 4 Paul thinks of righteousness as the gift of right relations which God bestows on the person who receives it in faith. Here, however, the righteousness which counts, and is therefore valid, is attributed to the person who combines belief with action.

2:25. Even a **harlot** (cf. Joshua 2:1-21) can be **justified**—that is, acquitted, excused, and made right—by actions which demonstrate true faith.

2:26. The conclusion is obvious. Faith and works, like **body** and **spirit,** are bound together. Faith without works, like a corpse without spirit, **is dead.**

VI. CONTROL THE TONGUE (3:1-12)

The opening verses of chapter 3 turn to a new subject without apparent transition from chapter 2. The author has previously mentioned controlling the tongue in 1:19, 26. He now develops and applies the theme more fully. His main point is: Control the tongue, for through it you also control the whole person. The second part of the argument (verses 6-12) is entirely negative. Not only is the tongue practically impossible to control, but the unbridled tongue leads to great disaster and self-perpetuating evil.

3:1-5. *The Tongue Controls the Person.* A widespread tendency is for people to appoint themselves as **teachers** and give advice to others. To be sure, there was need for teachers to instruct members of the church in New Testament times. Yet not all are qualified to teach. Here those who would teach are reminded that they have the greater responsibility since they will **be judged with greater strictness.**

3:2. The warning is particularly appropriate. **All** people— teachers included—**make many mistakes.** On the other hand, the person who does not make mistakes in speech is a mature person. The Greek words for **perfect man** can mean either a flawless person or a complete or whole person, one who is mature. Such maturity is shown in one's ability to control speech and **to bridle the whole body** as well.

3:3-4. Two obvious examples illustrate how the tongue, though small, is related to the control of the whole person. A bridle bit in the mouth of a horse controls its actions. Similarly, the small rudder of a great ship guides its direction at **the will of the pilot.**

3:5. The transition to the following discussion about the inability to control the tongue is formed by the warning that a **small fire**—in modern times, a match or lighted cigarette carelessly thrown away—can set a whole **forest . . . ablaze.**

3:6-12. *The Problem of the Tongue.* This passage points out the problem of the tongue, which is as deep as sin (though this word is not actually used). The difficulty is due to one's inability to control the tongue and the consequent impotence to control oneself. The author offers no solution to the problem except to exhort his readers, **This ought not to be so.**

3:6. The tongue, like a fire, rages with its evil effects in all parts of the **body.** In turn this fire is fed by the evil depths of human sickness. Hence it is perpetuated by the deep resources of **the cycle of nature.** That is, it sets in motion the force of human nature which is already sick and breeds corruption. The exact meaning of the text here is not clear. The alternate in the Revised Standard Version footnote, **wheel of birth,** could mean the force of heredity, not unlike "original sin." The flame is further nourished by the fire of **hell.** The Greek word for "hell" here is *Gehenna,* the city dump of Jerusalem. With its perpetual blaze this was a vivid reminder of the condemnation in the final judgment. In these references to the deep resources of evil the author is moving close to a doctrine of original sin and Paul's analysis of sin's power (cf. Romans 7).

3:7-8. The point here is obvious. The tongue, as related to the self, is a person's worst enemy. Wild beasts can be tamed. But one's own tongue, and consequently one's self, cannot be brought into subjection.

3:9-12. Further evidence of a person's lack of self-control is that the mouth pours forth both blessings and curses. These obvious contradictions indicate that something is radically wrong. In nature a **spring** does not yield both **fresh water** and brackish, nor does a **fig tree** bear **olives.** Only human beings have such a curious and disastrous contradiction in their nature. Thus the point of the exhortation remains: **This ought not to be so.**

VII. THE MEANING OF WISDOM (3:13-18)

The emphasis in this passage is on the meaning of true **wisdom,** which **comes down from above.** True wisdom stands in stark contrast to supposed earthly wisdom, which shows itself in **jealousy and selfish ambition,** leading to **disorder** and evil deeds.

The key word of the passage is **wisdom.** This is an important concept throughout the Bible and related writings, especially the so-called "wisdom literature" such as Proverbs, Wisdom of Solomon, and Ecclesiasticus. The word is frequently used with a wide variety of meanings. Sometimes it is used to designate prudence or worldly wisdom. Such earthly wisdom is often described in a bad sense and is contrasted with the wisdom of God—for example by Paul in I Corinthians 1–4, and in this passage.

3:13. True wisdom is a divine gift (verses 15, 17). Like faith, it is manifest in **good** patterns of **life,** in good **works,** and in virtues like **meekness** and those mentioned in verse 17.

3:14-16. The opposite of true wisdom is self-centeredness. This is characterized by **bitter jealousy and selfish ambition,** qualities of character which are nothing to boast about and are contrary to **truth.** Such supposed wisdom is earth-bound and even **devilish** or demonic.

3:17. Following a widespread custom of his day, the author lists the virtues which characterize the wisdom from above. Cf. Paul's contrast between works of the flesh and fruits of the spirit in Galatians 5:19-23.

3:18. This verse appears to be a teaching separated from its context. **Righteousness,** which to James means right conduct and piety (cf. 1:19-21; 2:21-23), is the fruit of **peace.** Seen in the context of the following passage, peace is the opposite of hostility and strife.

VIII. SUBMISSION TO GOD (4:1-17)

This chapter covers a wide range of subjects and appears to be loosely organized. But the basic theme running throughout is submission to God. This thought is brought into clear focus in verses 7-10, with the accent on God's exaltation of the humble in verse 10. In 2:14-26 the exhortation was aimed at those who think that religion consists in mere belief without good deeds. Chapter 4 is directed against those who are morally lax and still hold to worldly pleasures.

4:1-3. *Passions and Strife.* The strife mentioned in verses 1-2*ab* stands in contrast to righteousness and peace in 3:18. The author uses strong words to make his point: **wars, fightings,** and even **kill.** The root of these external ills is in the **passions** which rage in the **members** of the body. Such unchecked desires may lead to murder, and unquenched covetousness leads to conflict.

4:2c-3. It has already been said that God freely bestows gifts on those who ask in faith (1:5-6). Now the negative form of that teaching is stated: No one who asks **wrongly**—that is, simply to gratify **passions**—can receive anything. Here it is not lack of faith but wrong intention which cuts off the receiver from the gift (cf. 1:8).

4:4-6. *Love of the World Is Enmity with God.* The relationship between God and people throughout the Bible is based on a covenant of mutual fidelity (cf. Exodus 19; 24; Mark 14:24; Hebrews 9:15). Verses 4-10 seem to follow a threefold covenantal form:

    (1) warnings and curses against those who are unfaithful (verses 4-5);

    (2) blessings of grace to those who submit to God (verse 6);

    (3) obligations of the covenant people (verses 7-10).

4:4. The key to these verses is in the opening words, **unfaithful creatures.** Marital infidelity is the accusation, for the

Greek word means "adulteresses." The infidelity of God's
people is compared to adultery in Hosea 3:1, and Jesus
denounced his generation as adulterous and sinful (Mark 8:38).
Here a covenantal relationship of faithfulness between God and
the new people in Jesus Christ is assumed. Hence **friendship
with the world** can only mean a breach of covenant and **enmity
with God.** The "world" is everything which is corrupted by sin
and hence opposite, at enmity, with God (cf. 1:27; I John
2:15-17).

4:5-6. These verses are obscure and hard to interpret. **The
scripture** (literally "writing") can refer to a nonbiblical work as
well as the Old Testament. The quotation in verse 5 is not found
in the Old Testament and has not yet been found in other extant
writings. The Greek can mean either "Yearns jealously for him
the spirit" or **He yearns jealously over the spirit.** The latter
seems to fit the context better. **The spirit which he has made to
dwell in us** is probably an allusion to Genesis 2:7 and God's
desire for fellowship with men and women. The quotation in
verse 6 is from the Septuagint translation of Proverbs 3:34. It
serves as a text for the emphasis on **grace**—that is, God's gifts
and help to those who are humble.

4:7-10. *God Exalts the Humble.* The imperatives of this
passage are vigorous in moral fervor. Self-mortification stands in
contrast to passions and friendship with the world in verses 1-4.
It includes not only cleansing from sin and purification of the
heart but also **mourning** and **dejection.** Only those who thus
humble themselves will be exalted by God.

4:7-8a. Because God **gives grace to the humble** (verse 6), the
reader may well ask, "What shall we do?" The answer is, **Submit
yourselves . . . to God.** The meaning of submission is spelled
out in the following verses. The **devil** is the personification of
temptation to evil. That he **will flee** from those who resist is
spiritually and psychologically true. Those who have broken an
undesirable habit know that temptations weaken with persistent
resistance. Divine aid is avilable in the struggle against evil, for
God **will draw near** to those who come to God. (For other

examples of ways God or Christ helps the believer against sin cf. Romans 6:1-11; Ephesians 6:11-13 and Hebrews 2:18; 4:15-16).

4:8*b*-10. The injunction to **cleanse your hands** refers to ritual washing. It is interpreted in Isaiah 1:16-17 to mean changing from evil deeds to good and justice. "Clean hands and a pure heart" are combined in Psalm 24:4 as the prerequisite for approaching God. **Sinners** are **men of double mind** who would try to love both the world and God (verse 4; cf. 1:8). To the author repentance means that worldly pleasure and wickedness must be rejected. Christians must mortify themselves so that their **laughter** turns to **mourning** and **joy to dejection** (cf. Luke 6:25). These disciplines are not ends in themselves, however, for God exalts those who thus **humble** themselves (cf. verse 6).

4:11-12. *Judge Not.* That the Christian should not **speak evil against . . . another** or judge a **brother** is a universal New Testament teaching. The author points out how this practice amounts to opposing **the law,** for in this way the judge is placed above the law. Here, as in 1:25 and 2:8-12, law means the law of God revealed in the Old Testament and interpreted by Jesus and Christian tradition.

4:12. Where the law of God is concerned, there is but **one lawgiver and judge,** God. God has the will and power **to save and to destroy.** Though the author does not quote the words of Jesus, he echoes the Lord's teaching in Matthew 10:28.

4:13-17. *Living Under God's Care.* Under normal circumstances life appears to have a certain permanence. A businessman comes to assume that tomorrow he can buy, sell, and travel just as he did today (verse 13). Such confidence is unfounded. It is like that of the man with a bumper crop who plans to build bigger barns to store his grain so he may rest in his assumed security. His assumption is false, and he is a fool (Luke 12:13-21). Such a person does not realize that life is but a **mist,** like a breath on a cold morning which appears for less than a second. The realization of the conditional nature of human life—**if the Lord wills**—is the beginning and constant state of living under God's care.

4:16. The recognition of life's conditional nature rules out

boasting (cf. Paul's affirmation that faith excludes boasting, Romans 3:27). All such **arrogance,** like worldliness, is **evil.**

4:17. The name which might be given to all forms of evil in this chapter is **sin.** The definition here is thoroughly practical and has to do with deeds. To know the right and to fail in doing it is sin. This practical concept of sin is less profound than that of Paul, who understands the deepest dimensions of the biblical view. For Paul, sin is a power that works in every person. Only God's miraculous deliverance in Christ can liberate and enable one to live a new kind of life (Romans 7).

IX. AGAINST RICHES AND INJUSTICE (5:1-6)

Throughout the letter the author has opposed the rich and favored the poor. He has warned the wealthy that life is transient and that riches will pass away (1:9-11). He has accused the rich of oppressing Christians and of blasphemy (2:6-7). Here he expands on these themes in two ways, by showing that the rich:

(1) are headed for miseries, especially those of the last days;
(2) have gained their wealth by committing injustice, particularly against agricultural workers.

5:1-3. *Wealth Is Corrupted.* Probably the **rich** are not members of Christian congregations. But the indictment is general and is hurled at the rich as a class. They are warned to **weep and howl** because of the **miseries** about to come upon them. These are signs of the coming judgment and the **last days** (verse 3).

5:2-3. The verbs **have rotted, are** (literally "have become") **moth-eaten,** and **have rusted** are in the perfect tense to show that though these corruptions are still in the future, their effects are as good as already accomplished. The last days have already begun. Even the most permanent forms of earthly wealth, like **gold and silver,** have no eternal value. Looked at from the viewpoint of the last days, they too are subject to corrosion.

Far from having real value, these precious metals stand as

evidence (literally "witness") against the rich. These people have failed to care for the poor as prescribed in Deuteronomy 15:7-8 and probably have gained their wealth through injustice (cf. verses 4-6). Riches alone cannot satisfy. Consequently people who seek wealth for its own sake find that its corruption will consume them—**will eat your flesh like fire.** Most translations punctuate verse 3 with a period after **fire,** leaving the following sentence fragmented and obscure. The Revised Standard Version footnote indicates an alternate translation: "will eat your flesh, since you have stored up fire for the last days." This makes clear that the fire is that of the final judgment which the rich store up for themselves. The rich person is headed for disappointment in this life and judgment in the life to come (cf. Matthew 6:19-20).

5:4-6. *Injustice Cries Out.* From ancient times down to American migratory workers and sharecroppers, agricultural laborers have been among the most exploited of peoples. Legislation in the Old Testament insisted that workers be paid promptly and fairly (Deuteronomy 24:14-15) lest injustice against laborers **cry out** to the **Lord of hosts,** the avenger of the poor.

5:5. Those who in this life live in **luxury and pleasure** simply fatten themselves like cattle for the **slaughter**—that is, the judgment—which is at hand.

5:6. The rich and the powerful **have condemned** and **have killed the righteous man.** The **righteous man** is identical with the poor (cf. Amos 2:6-7; 5:12; 8:4). He does not resist injustices against him because it would be folly to do so.

X. PATIENT WAITING FOR THE LORD (5:7-12)

5:7-11. *Patience and Steadfastness.* From the threat of judgment against the rich the author now turns to exhort the Christian **brethren** to be patient while awaiting the **coming of the Lord.** In early New Testament times the *parousia,* or arrival, of the Lord was expected in the immediate future. The apparent delay of his return caused some problems of impatience and misunderstanding among Christians (cf. Matthew 24:3-6; 1 Thessalonians 4:13-18; I John 2:28).

5:9. The period of waiting may try the patience of some. They may be tempted to **grumble** or blame each other for their troubles. Since they may thus fall into judgment, they are warned that the Lord who comes is like a judge who stands at the door.

5:10-11. Further examples of **suffering and patience** are found in the **prophets.** Because they **spoke in the name of the Lord,** they were persecuted. Similarly, **Job** was steadfast, even when tried with severe pain and great losses. Yet in the final outcome God did show him mercy and compassion. Such an end is a token of God's purpose, an additional incentive for waiting with patience.

5:12. *Do Not Swear.* This verse has no apparent connection with the preceding or following passages. The injunction against oaths is found in the teaching of Jesus (Matthew 5:33-37) and often in Jewish writings. The point of the saying is simply that the Christian should always speak the truth. Both his **yes** and his **no** should mean what they say. No oath can or should make a Christian truthful, nor can the lack of an oath permit one to lie. With anything less than the truth one falls into **condemnation.**

XI. MINISTERING TO EACH OTHER (5:13-20)

This is one of the most positive sections in the whole book. In the language of the modern church the passage describes the "priesthood of all believers." It shows ways in which Christians minister to each other. Specific practices in the modern church may differ from those of New Testament times, but the concern of Christians to serve one another in the fellowship of the church is the same.

5:13-15. *The Service of Prayer.* In life's experiences Christians know **suffering** or trouble as well as good times when they can be **cheerful.** In all circumstances of life they can and should turn to God. In suffering Christians should **pray;** in fortunate circumstances they should **sing praise.**

5:14-15. In verse 14 **sick** refers to illness rather than to suffering or trouble as in verse 13. When a church member is sick, he is to **call for the elders of the church.** Undoubtedly the organizational structure of early Christian communities was patterned after that of the Jewish synagogues. The office of **elder** has a long history in Judaism. In New Testament times each Jewish community had its council of elders. The references to elders in the church of Jerusalem (Acts 11:30; 15:2, 4, 6, 22-23; 16:4; 21:18) suggest that they functioned much like elders in Jewish communities.

Distinctive in this passage, however, is the fact that the elders perform a ministry of prayer and anointing for the sick. They are not simply governing authorities or organizational leaders but functioning ministers to members of the congregation.

The elders are to **pray over** the sick man—that is, at his bedside, and they should anoint him **with oil in the name of the Lord.** Since Mark 6:13 is the only other place in the New Testament which mentions anointing as a rite in healing, the practice was probably not widespread among the churches. Verse 14 recommends both prayers of the elders and their anointing the sick man. But verse 15 stresses the **prayer of faith**—a prayer offered without doubt (cf. 1:6)—as the element which will **save the sick man** or heal him from his sickness (cf. verse 20, **will save his soul**) because **the Lord will raise him up.**

But restoration to physical health alone falls short of real cure. The forgiveness of sins is necessary for the total well-being and wholeness of the person (cf. Mark 2:5). The healing ministry of the church has as its objective the cure of souls, the restoration of health to the whole person.

5:16-18. *Confession and Intercession.* In the ongoing ministry of the church the elders do not function alone. Rather, Christians minister to one another and are urged to **confess** their **sins** to each other. But there is an immediate return to prayer, the dominant theme of the passage. In the context of mutual confession and prayer, healing takes place in the fellowship of the church.

5:17-18. To illustrate his conclusion in verse 16 the author cites the example of Elijah (I Kings 17:1; 18:1, 42-45). He prophesied to King Ahab that rain would cease until the word of the Lord would command it to fall again. The rain did cease and only began again when Elijah bowed himself down to the earth. Interestingly, the author cites the incident of the drought rather than Elijah's healing of the widow's son (I Kings 17:17-24) and he does not mention the healing miracles of Jesus. His main point is that Elijah, a mere man—**of like nature with ourselves**—prayed and his prayers were answered. If the prayers of this righteous man effected a drought, how much more will the prayers of Christians avail for health and salvation.

5:19-20. *Bring Back Wanderers.* In primitive Christianity doctrines were not fully defined, and Christians were subject to severe trials (1:2-4) and temptations to worldliness (4:1-10). The tendency to wander from the truth was a real problem. To bring back such wanderers was part of the church's ministry. The person who **brings back a sinner from the error of his way**—back into the fellowship of the church as described in verses 13-18—**will save his soul from death and will cover a multitude of sins** (cf. the familiar saying in I Peter 4:8 that "love covers a multitude of sins"). The meaning of this is ambiguous. Will the person who brings back the wanderer save his *own* soul and thus cover a multitude of his own sins? Or will his action save the soul of the wanderer and cover his sins? Probably the latter is correct. The wanderer can be made whole when he comes back into fellowship with the church, where he can join again in confession and prayer (verse 16).

The author does not mention the atoning work of Christ which covers sins. Rather his focus is on the church where that atoning work is known and shared. The church knows the forgiveness of sins in a fellowship of confession and prayer. The return of the wanderer **will cover a multitude of sins**—his own, those of the person who brings him back, and those of the whole Christian fellowship, where forgiveness of sins is a shared reality.

THE FIRST LETTER OF PETER

Claude Holmes Thompson

INTRODUCTION

This vigorous letter has long been a favorite in the church. Addressed to Christians in Asia Minor, it sought to encourage them as they faced scorn from their neighbors and, to some extent, persecution from the government. Authorship, date, purpose, and theology are all bound up together.

Authorship

Though the text designates Peter the apostle as the author, serious questions have been raised against this claim. It is said that

(1) the rugged Galilean fisherman could not have written the exquisite Greek of this letter;

(2) it refers to persecutions more intense than any which took place by the time of Peter's death around A.D. 64;

(3) it relies too heavily upon the letters of Paul, which allegedly were not circulated extensively until after Peter's death;

(4) it shows little evidence of the personal acquaintance Peter had with Jesus.

In reply, several points must be considered.

(1) The excellent Greek may be due to Silvanus, the "Silas" of

Acts and the Silvanus of II Corinthians 1:19; I Thessalonians 1:1; and II Thessalonians 1:1. This responsible member of the church in Jerusalem, a Roman citizen and fellow missioner with Paul, could have written the letter for Peter, as stated in 5:12.

(2) The persecutions need not refer to those under the emperor Trajan in A.D. 111-112. Very early the church was mistreated for bearing the name "Christian" (Acts 5:41; 9:16; 21:13). By about A.D. 50 Paul met trouble in Thessalonica (I Thessalonians 2:14-15). The report in this letter could reflect the gathering storm under Nero (A.D. 54-68).

(3) As for the influence of Paul, much of this material was common property of the Christian community before he began to write about A.D. 51. Peter had access to the same material, and he likely had seen Paul's letter to Rome, written perhaps between A.D. 53-58.

(4) The absence of firsthand knowledge of the life of Jesus seems overstated. The author claims to have seen Jesus (1:8) and to have witnessed his sufferings (5:1). The Master's teachings echo in various places in the letter (1:13, 17; 2:12; 3:9, 14; 4:5, 14; 5:2, 6-7).

Yet different judgments remain concerning authorship. The case against Peter as the author has not been established. If we accept the contribution of Sylvanus, the view that Peter produced the letter may be accepted.

Date and Place of Composition

If the letter was the joint work of Peter and Silvanus, it may be dated around 64—not long before Peter lost his life and shortly before the outbreak of the persecution under Nero. Since loyalty to the emperor is urged (2:13-17), doubtless that persecution, while anticipated, had not yet begun.

An early date is suggested also by the absence of technical language pertaining to church organization. The only term referring to church officials is "elder" (5:1). Not even the familiar terms "deacon" and "bishop" are used.

There seems no reason to reject the traditional view that this letter was written from Rome. This city was referred to as

"Babylon," a term recognized among Christians as the designation of the capital city of the empire (5:13; cf. Revelation 14:8; 16:19; 17:5; 18:2, 10, 21).

Purpose

I Peter appears to have one major purpose with several secondary, though closely related, emphases. The basic theme is to provide encouragement now that persecution seems imminent. Even in so brief a letter persecution is mentioned at least four times (1:6-7; 3:16-17; 4:12-19; 5:9). One element of encouragement is the promise of the return of Christ. This is referred to quite vividly (1:5, 7, 13; 2:12; 4:13, 17; 5:1, 4). The purpose is to keep hope alive at any cost—but it is hope which only God can vindicate.

There seems to be some liturgical purpose in the letter, especially in reference to baptism and Holy Communion. It may be that 1:3–4:11 is a manual of instruction for new converts, with 2:4-10 and 3:18-22 included as hymns of encouragement. At least the author intends to instruct his readers in the faith.

There is also an ethical purpose. The new life through baptism is a radical departure from the old patterns of conduct. Not only are there specific instructions for husbands, wives, and servants. There is clear evidence that the believers in Christ are to be obviously different from their pagan neighbors (1:14; 2:1, 9, 11-18; 3:1, 7; 4:3-6, 15). But the total purpose of the letter involves the certain grace of God as available for any need (5:12).

Theology

God is the "faithful Creator" (4:19) who is likewise "the God and Father of our Lord Jesus Christ" (1:3). God's gracious care extends to all people (5:7, 10). But God is righteous in all judgments, since divine judgments rest upon God's own holy character (1:14-17). Thus God is both "for" the righteous and "against" the wicked (5:5), yet God's patience in dealing with the wicked demonstrates the quality of holy compassion (3:20). While God's people may endure suffering here on earth (3:17; 4:19), they are to submit to the Lord, knowing that God will give strength for the day and assurance of final victory for the future (5:6, 10).

The doctrine concerning Christ is related also to this certainty of suffering (1:11), but these sufferings are redemptive (3:18). While Christ is set forth as an "example" (2:21), he is likewise to be worshiped as "Lord" (3:15). Peter here reflects the earliest creed of the church which can be seen also in Paul (cf. Romans 10:9; 14:9: I Corinthians 12:3; Philippians 2:11). As Lord Jesus Christ is the standard for final judgment (2:7-8; 4:5). This lordship is more than the portrait of a good man committed to his ideals. Jesus is seen as a redeeming sacrifice unique in human history.

While the word "church" is not in the letter, three definitive ideas of the church are present: "spiritual house" (2:5), "God's own people" (2:9), and "flock of God" (5:2). The whole theology is primitive. That is, it is centered in the earliest proclamation of the gospel. All the elements in the *kerygma,* or proclamation, are found clearly stated. But there is also the clearly defined *didache,* or instruction in Christian living. Thus here is the earliest stratum of Christian witness.

I. GREETING AND PRAISE (1:1-9)

1:1-2. *The Author's Greeting.* The author identifies himself as **Peter, an apostle of Jesus Christ.** It is obvious that he intended to include himself among the twelve. In Aramaic, the dialect spoken by the Jews of the time, Peter's name was Simon Bar-Jona, or Simon son of John. But Jesus had given him the additional name of Cephas, or "Rock," which was to convey a symbolic meaning later in the life of this yet unsteady disciple. Since this letter is addressed to Greek-speaking Jews, it is natural that it should carry the Greek form of the name, Petros.

In a sense Peter is his Christian name. Just as Paul does not use his original name of Saul in his letters, so Peter uses this distinctive Christian form to refer to himself.

The language of the opening phrase could simply mean one

sent on a special mission. But here it obviously is used to designate Peter as an authentic apostle, an originally appointed member of the twelve. Though at times Paul had to defend his apostleship, Peter apparently feels his clear claim to this authority will be accepted by his readers.

To the exiles of the Dispersion in Greek actually reads, "to the elect strangers of the Dispersion." The idea of election, once held to refer to Israel alone, now is applied to all the redeemed under the new covenant of grace (cf. 2:9 with Deuteronomy 7:6).

The Dispersion technically refered to Jews living outside Palestine. Here it is used not only to designate Christians alienated from their native land but also to indicate the temporal nature of this exile. Thus while the Christians were the new Israel, they were also the new Dispersion.

Pontus, Galatia, Cappadocia, Asia, and **Bithynia** are districts in northern Asia Minor. They were important in early Christianity, especially in the ministry of Paul and in Revelation (cf. Acts 2:9; 16:6-7; 18:2; I Corinthians 16:1; Galatians; Revelation 1–3). It is significant that within about three decades of the crucifixion the church was sufficiently strong in this remote area of the Roman Empire to warrant this letter.

1:2. Destined by God the Father is literally "according to the foreknowledge of God the Father." Apparently many translators have felt that the stronger terms, "destined," or "predestined," are implied in the Semitic idiom, where "to foreknow" means much the same as "to determine" or "to decide." This idea underscores the divinely **chosen** mission of these believers. If they were mostly slaves—as seems possible—this must have given them an exciting sense of dignity.

This divine election is the first of three definitive elements of Christian living set forth. The second is that of being **sanctified by the Spirit.** Basically this ministry of the Holy Spirit is threefold:

    (1) to purify the church redeemed by Christ,

    (2) to set it apart as a distinct fellowship of believers,

    (3) to empower it to continue to witness to the ministry begun by Christ and consummated by his death and resurrection.

The third element refers to the purpose of this divine election and sanctification: **for obedience to Jesus Christ and for sprinkling with his blood.** Here the inauguration of the new covenant through Christ is seen in the light of the old covenant made at Sinai (Exodus 24:7-8).

The trinitarian form of these expressions—**Father . . . Spirit . . . Jesus Christ**—has been mentioned by various writers. We must not read back into this letter the doctrine of the Holy Trinity, which was formulated in the midst of later controversy. Yet this is what has been called a "trinity of experience."

The salutation concludes with words almost identical with those used by Paul: **May grace and peace be multiplied to you.** Grace is God's suffering love in action, redeeming sinful people who do not deserve this unmerited gift. Peace is practically identical with the idea of salvation.

1:3-9. *The Doxology of New Life.* Two ideas dominate these verses—a doxology for the risen Savior and the certainty of new life in Christ. Writing to frightened people whom he knows face trials, Peter gives encouragement through praise to God. The source of the Christian's strength is the power of the resurrection of the Lord—now available. **Blessed** is not used in the same sense as in the Beatitudes (Matthew 5; Luke 6). In the Sermon on the Mount the word describes the happiness, the bliss, of the person in communion with God. But here the word is used in prayer addressed to God. The simplest Jewish prayer, "Blessed art Thou, O God," becomes, **Blessed be the God and Father of our Lord Jesus Christ!** Yahweh, somewhat remote, even austere, is now intimate and personal in Jesus Christ.

1:3. The theme of rebirth is a major message of the New Testament. Nicodemus needs to be "born of the Spirit" (John 3:6). The believer walks in "newness of life" (Romans 6:4). The Christian is a "new creation" (II Corinthians 5:17). While once we were dead in sin, we have now been "made . . . alive together with Christ" (Ephesians 2:5). The **living hope** to which Peter refers is rooted in **the resurrection of Jesus Christ from the dead.** His resurrection not only guarantees our resurrection. It also keeps hope fresh and alive until we join him in the life beyond the reach of death. The certainty of the resurrection of Christ from the dead was the central theme of all preaching in the early church.

1:4-5. This hope is nurtured by **an inheritance . . . imperishable, undefiled, and unfading.** In the Septuagint "inheritance" refers to Canaan, the land of promise. Peter uses the same word here. Thus this inheritance is **kept in heaven for you** as a kind of heavenly Canaan. But since **the last time** has already entered history in the ministry of Christ, who "was made manifest at the end of the times" (1:20), the Christian already has a foretaste and guarantee of this blessed hope. This inheritance is reserved **in heaven** untouched by earthly changes. Those who are to receive it are **guarded through faith** until its final possession.

1:5-9. Salvation is used to indicate divine action in the past, humanity's present experience, and the future hope. Since the Christians were already living **in the last time,** they could **rejoice** in spite of impending trials. Suffering is the lot of the faithful, as of the Lord. Yet this only serves to distinguish genuine faith from sham. Peter contrasts his own experience of having known Jesus "in the flesh" with his readers, who were not so privileged. Yet so authentic was Jesus' mission they could still love him and believe in him (cf. John 20:29*b*).

II. A LIVING HOPE (1:10-25)

1:10-12. *From the Prophets to the Gospel.* The Bible of the first Christians was the Old Testament, and the importance of the prophets can hardly be overstated. The early church saw the uncompleted hopes of the prophetic movement. Thus it was inevitable that these Old Testament writers should be read so as to foreshadow the coming of the Messiah. This is a common New Testament theme. Jesus said that the prophets looked for the day which Peter is describing "and did not see it" (Matthew 13:17).

Four things seem significant in this relation of the gospel to the prophetic insights:

(1) The **prophets** did not passively receive an imposed message—**they searched and inquired about this salvation.**

(2) It was **the Spirit of Christ within them.** That is, the secret both of the ministry of Jesus and of the prophets was the Spirit of God.

(3) Christ is understood as the Suffering Servant. The early Christians understood that Jesus identified his ministry with that of the Suffering Servant of Isaiah (cf. Luke 22:37 with Isaiah 53:12; Acts 8:32-33 with Isaiah 53:7-8; Hebrews 9:28 with Isaiah 53:12).

(4) They knew their vision was not for their own day but for the time of fulfillment. That time had now come.

1:13-21. *An Admonition.* Peter now turns to the consequences in Christian living. As the oriental worker wearing flowing robes must tuck up the loose ends under a belt, so in Christian living there must be no frazzled ends, no fuzzy thinking. Christians must **gird up** their **minds.** A modern metaphor might be: "Roll up your sleeves."

Be sober is a warning not to panic even though trouble does come. Strenuous discipline is required of the believer. But what is the basis of this appeal? Five elements seem apparent.

(1) **1:14-16.** First is the call to sanctity. As God is **holy,** so must his children be. Peter, appealing to Leviticus 11:44-45, sets the standard as conformity to the character of God. This is both negative—**do not be conformed** to the old way (cf. Romans 12:2)—and positive—**be holy yourselves in all your conduct.** Then as now, the standard for Christian living is still holiness of character and conduct.

(2) **1:17.** Second, there is the judgment of God. **Conduct yourselves with fear,** since we now live in **exile** on earth. The reference is to the impartial judgment of God upon the children of Israel during their stay in the wilderness.

(3) **1:18-21.** Third is the tremendous cost of redemption. **The precious blood of Christ** is responsible for this rescue from bondage. **Blood** refers to the poured out, or spilled, blood, as in

ceremonial sacrifices. Here Christ is seen as the Passover Lamb slain from **before the foundation of the world** (cf. Ephesians 1:4-10; Revelation 13:8).

(4) **1:20.** Fourth, an idea expressed in verse 5—"revealed in the last time"—is given somewhat fuller treatment: **He was . . . made manifest at the end of the times.** The coming of Christ has been the beginning of the end. With the incarnation the kingdom has been inaugurated. The final stage of human history under God is on its way. However, there will still be a final consummation in the "revelation of Jesus Christ" (verses 7, 13). But these two ideas are inseparable.

(5) **1:21.** Finally, the appearance of Christ on earth produces faith, especially since God **raised him from the dead.** The life, death, and resurrection constitute what is sometimes spoken of as "the Christ-event." This faith is not the creation by an adoring church. No mythological Jesus can account for it.

1:22-25. *Brotherhood of the New Birth.* There is community through social or political structures as within a state. There is community through natural generation as in a family. But here Peter describes a community through divine grace, by rebirth into the family of God.

1:22-23. Peter's reference to **obedience to the truth** is regarded as referring to baptism, initiation into the Christian way. It results in moral sanctification, which in turn is seen as Christian love within the fellowship. But this love is not simply good will. It comes from the completely transformed life which Peter refers to as being **born anew.**

1:23-25. This new life comes through **imperishable** divine **seed** which is identified with **the living and abiding word of God.** Those so reborn become "partakers of the divine nature" (II Peter 1:4). But this word of God is no mere collection of written documents. It is God's message of salvation declared for all people. Peter contrasts the transitoriness of life through natural descent with the permanence of this divine rebirth. "That which is born of the flesh is flesh" (John 3:6) and hence is subject to decay. But "that which is born of the spirit is spirit" (John 3:6) and hence **abides for ever.**

III. NEW LIFE IN CHRIST (2:1-12)

2:1-3. *New Birth Means New Life.* "Love of the brethren" (1:22) requires the elimination of characteristics of the old life. Some of these well-known evils are stated. Peter indicates that new life cannot continue along with these death-producing practices. They must be stripped off with relentless severity.

2:2-3. But positively, this new life needs nourishment. An automatic function of the newly born infant is eating. The word here for **newborn babes** refers to infants in arms, hence the metaphor is appropriate. Does this suggest that the readers were recent converts? Perhaps. A similar idea is used by Paul regarding the Corinthian Christians (I Corinthians 3:1-2). The writer of Hebrews blames the people for their continued infancy (Hebrews 5:12-14). But here Peter sees this healthy appetite as a good thing, provided it is satisfied with proper food.

2:4-10. *The New People of God.* The new people were not merely individual Christians. They were the church. By the use of figures of speech, Old Testament references, and personal appeals, the origin, nature, and function of the church are set forth.

The origin is Christ, **in Zion a stone, a cornerstone** (cf. Isaiah 28:16). Though **rejected by men,** he **has become the head of the corner,** since he was divinely **chosen.** This divine choice brings judgment, since he is **a stone that will make men stumble, a rock that will make them fall** (cf. Isaiah 8:14). This stumbling comes from disobedience to the will of God.

The nature of the church is suggested in the metaphor of the **spiritual house** constructed of the **living stones** of believers. But this spiritual house is further described as a **race, . . . priesthood, . . . nation, . . . people.** This is one of the most meaningful interpretations of the church in the New Testament. Note that all terms are corporate. To be a Christian is to live within the community of God's people.

These descriptive terms all come from the Old Testament. As with Israel, the church is the new race to inherit the role of the elect people. As Jesus is the Messiah, king of the new kingdom, his subjects are a priesthood. They continue the role of Israel as the priestly people. The word *laos,* from which comes laity, refers to all the people who belong to God, as distinct from all others. These were the new people of the new covenant.

The function of the church is to **declare the wonderful deeds** of God's redeeming love by offering **spiritual sacrifices acceptable to God through Jesus Christ.**

Three contrasts should be noted in this discussion of the church:

(1) Though Christ was rejected by those to whom he came, he was divinely chosen. This same idea is seen in Peter's sermon at Pentecost.

(2) God called the people **out of darkness into his marvelous light.** The conflict between light and darkness is a common New Testament theme.

(3) There is a contrast between **no people** and **God's people.** This is an obvious reference to Hosea 1:6, 9 and 2:23.

2:11-12. *Pilgrims Among Pagans.* These words introduce a discussion concerning the Christian's conduct within a pagan society. Peter had warned against sins of the inner life. Now he speaks of **passions of the flesh.** While these may be crude physical practices, they are primarily the perverted condition of human life, the "fallenness" of unredeemed human nature, the self twisted inward and away from God. Thus there is warfare between the old life and the new. This is a common theme in Paul's writings (cf. Romans 7:7–8:14 and Galatians 5:6-25).

Like the children of Israel, Christians know they are aliens and exiles on earth. But they are not thereby excused from noble conduct. Negatively, there is the demand to avoid the desires of the flesh, the lower nature. Positively, behavior must be such as to impress even the pagans with the excellence of the Christian way. **So that . . . they may see your good deeds** seems an obvious reference to the saying of Jesus: "Let your light so shine before men, that they may see your good works and give glory to your Father who is in heaven" (Matthew 5:16).

IV. CHRISTIAN RELATIONSHIPS (2:13–3:17)

2:13-17. *Church and State.* Christians may not ignore their responsibility as citizens. This section regards the state as a divine institution, designed to protect the weak, punish the unruly, and provide welfare for all. Life is to be an ordered society, not chaos.

2:16. Acting as **free men** and at the same time as **servants of God** is the paradox of Christian living within the state. Freedom does not mean unrestrained liberty to do as one may please. Rather, it is freedom to do the will of God.

2:17. The author gives four short rules for Christians to follow in their relationships with one another and with non-Christians.

(1) They must **honor all men,** for each is a person for whom Christ died. No one is cheap, not one of the sixty million slaves of Rome. This idea was a breath of fresh Christian air in a land where multitudes were exploited.

(2) Christians must **love the brotherhood.** Within the Christian fellowship is born a new relationship which reflects the kind of God-caring love which led Jesus to die for sinners.

(3) They must **fear God**—fear in the sense of reverence, awe, worship.

(4) Finally they must **honor the emperor.** If this emperor was Nero, Peter calls for an attitude by the church which even some Romans could not endorse.

2:18-25. *Suffering Servants.* The word for **servants** used here refers to household, or domestic, servants. Slavery was a recognized fact in the early church. Many Christians were slaves. But in spite of this there is no evidence that the gospel sought the destruction of this social system. It was accepted, and directions were given for its operation. Slaves were often people of culture and education, at times superior to their masters. Doctors, librarians, teachers, musicians, and secretaries were among them. Slaves had no legal rights at all. They were not people; they were things. Sooner or later the implicit freedom for every person would emerge. But when Peter wrote this letter, this was far in the future.

2:18-20. Servants are to obey—not only when masters are considerate, but also when they are cruel. Thus if servants could not please their masters, they at least could please their God, who understood their plight. Their motive of service, therefore, was not to curry favor with these masters, but to **have God's approval.** God honors **suffering** which comes **unjustly.** On the other hand, pain which comes from wrongdoing is simply what is deserved.

2:21-25. But why is suffering meritorious? **Because Christ also suffered for you, leaving you an example, that you should follow in his steps.** These verses should be read in the light of Isaiah 53, where the figure of the Suffering Servant is seen. Cf. especially parallel expressions in Isaiah 53:5-6, 9, 12. This messianic passage was understood in the church to portray the divine purpose in the death of Christ. It sees Christ's death as God's answer to human sin.

The significance of this message for slaves must not be overlooked. Christ's suffering is not only redemptive. It is an **example** which even slaves are to imitate. His patience under mistreatment, suffering without threats, death in behalf even of enemies, could not fail to impress those called to endure unjust treatment. God would bring justice to cruel masters. The death of Christ brought healing to those who had to suffer. It was also the means of bringing straying ones to the **Shepherd** who would forever be the **Guardian of** their **souls.** The word used here for "guardian" is often translated "bishop." But apparently Peter uses it for Christ's ministry of protecting his chosen ones. It has no reference to ecclesiastical office.

3:1-7. *Wives and Husbands.* In this section there are six verses for instruction to wives, one verse for husbands. **Wives,** like servants, had little standing in the ancient world. Hence the need for more detailed directions concerning their conduct. Husbands, when they became Christians, took their wives with them into the fellowship of the church. But if wives became Christians, their husbands did not necessarily follow them. Thus there was need for special care in their manner of life. They are to be obedient even to a pagan husband. This may lead to the conversion of the husband. But even if it does not, they must still be obedient. Peter appeals to the example of **Sarah,** who **obeyed Abraham,** in support of his directive for submission.

3:2. The standard of chastity, **chaste behavior,** is of special significance. It has been said that the one unique virtue which Christianity contributed to the ancient world was chastity. There was a single pattern for Christian conduct for men or women—moral purity (James 1:27).

3:3-6. As for dress, Peter warns against luxury, show, and even excessive attention given to the **hair** styles currently in vogue.

3:7. Husbands too have a responsibility. They are not to exploit their superior physical powers but to recognize that along with their wives they share a common life within the grace of God. This has been referred to as spiritual equality (cf. Ephesians 5:25-33; Colossians 3:19). In addition Peter suggests that unless husbands recognize this **joint** participation of both sexes in a spiritual fellowship, a meaningful prayer life is impossible.

In the ancient world a woman had an inferior position. She, like the slave, was not a person but a thing, a piece of property. Theoretically, Christianity changed all this by destroying the inferior status of women. Peter exalts the realtionship of husband and wife as a noble expression of Christianity at its best. This was important at a time when questions had been raised concerning the wisdom of marriage at all, in view of the shortness of the time (I Corinthians 7:7-8, 20, 26-27).

3:8-12. *Christian Action and Attitude.* Christian attitudes which promote Christian conduct are presented here. Christian **unity** leaves no place for quarrels and divisions. This is a basic New Testament idea. Jesus prays for it (John 17:21-23), and the church early experienced it (Acts 4:32). Paul repeatedly urges it. This is not to be a flat and uncritical uniformity in which personal differences are erased. Rather, it is fellowship beyond these differences.

3:8. A close relation exists between **sympathy** and **love of the brethren.** We have to have love for one another which will

93

express itself in a suffering concern, a sympathy which has no room for selfishness. **A tender heart** means compassionate concern for the suffering people of the world. **A humble mind** suggests teachableness, but it also refers to the kind of humility seen in Jesus (Matthew 11:29; 23:12). Peter must have written these words with painful memories of his own weaknesses, yet with humble gratitude for God's mercy.

3:9-12. Forgiveness, the refusal to pay back **evil for evil,** means there is no place for retaliation in the Christian life. Verses 10-12 are based on Psalm 34, which is used freely to show the contrast between one who merits God's approval and the one who does not.

3:13-17. *The Christian in Trouble.* Does Peter here recall the words of Jesus: "Blessed are those who are persecuted for righteousness' sake, for theirs is the kingdom of heaven" (Matthew 5:10)?

3:15-16. To **reverence Christ as Lord** reflects the earliest Christian creed, "Jesus is Lord" (cf. Romans 10:9; I Corinthians 12:3; Philippians 2:11). "Lord" is used in the Septuagint for God, and here the divine title is assigned to Jesus. This confession provides a freedom from fear of suffering. It also provides a basis for witness. So often suffering and a **defense** of the faith go together. The confession, however, must be made **with gentleness and reverence,** no arrogance or abuse. After all, the best evidence is **good behavior in Christ.**

3:17. Sometimes this witness brings pain. But while suffering for wrong is the consequence of faulty living, suffering for the right may indeed be the **will** of God.

V. CHRIST THE SAVIOR (3:18–4:19)

3:18-20. *The Suffering Savior.* This passage requires careful attention. Several themes are crucial.

3:18. The first of these themes reveals the meaning of the death of Christ. The cosmic character of that death is seen in his passion on earth, his ministry among the departed spirits beyond death (verse 19), and his consequent authority in heaven (verse 22). Whatever else he thought of Christ, the author could never understand him as only a man among people. And even if verse 18 reads "suffered" instead of **died,** as some manuscripts have it, the context carries the same redemptive meaning. His death was unique, **once for all,** never requiring repetition.

Again, it was death **for sins.** It was a divine atonement to restore a broken relationship between God and humanity. Likewise, it was vicarious, **the righteous for the unrighteous.** It removed the barrier between sinful humans and the holy God—**that he might bring us to God**—since "through him we . . . have access in one Spirit to the Father" (Ephesians 2:18).

The expression, **being put to death in the flesh but made alive in the spirit,** probably refers to the death of the earthly flesh which Jesus took in the Incarnation and to the quickening of his own self (spirit) for his continued ministry beyond the resurrection.

3:19-20. The second theme is Christ's ministry to the dead. These verses, with parallel thoughts in 4:6, suggest that Jesus, after crucifixion and before resurrection, proclaimed the gospel to those who had died before his time. Thus even the departed souls in Hades are confronted by the claims of Christ. This passage lies back of the expression in the Apostles' Creed, "He descended into hell."

3:20-22. The third theme concerns Christ's ministry in heaven. These verses tie together a series of ideas:

(1) Noah was rescued from an evil people **through water.**

(2) Water suggests **baptism,** the saving sacrament for the Christian.

(3) Baptism is meaningful only because **through the resurrection of Jesus Christ** the believer is raised to a new life.

(4) Resurrection has led to Christ's priestly function **at the right hand of God.** Thus the authority of Christ extends from before the covenant with Abraham to his final rule in **heaven.**

4:1-6. *Through Death to Life.* This section now returns to the thought in 3:18. As Paul indicates in Romans 6:3-14, baptism is seen as a dying to the sin of the present life to live a new life in Christ. The new life and the old are contrasted as **human passions** and **the will of God.** These are the alternatives which are spelled out quite vividly. Cf. the specific evils with Paul's list of the "works of the flesh" in Galatians 5:19-21. The lofty ethical standards of the Christian community stood in contrast to the sordidness of the time. This is seen as an eschatological judgment, since God **is ready to judge the living and the dead.** The final judgment between right and wrong has come in Christ. It is now about to be seen within the Christian community.

4:7-11. *The Beginning of the End.* In the New Testament there is a persistent note of something just about to happen. The Christian always lives on the edge of the end. The final judgment has already come. There is no judgment more final than the entrance of Christ into history.

These verses refer to sanity, sobriety, prayerfulness, **love,** and **hospitality** with joy. These are the qualities of Christian life at the beginning of **the end.** In light of the shaky minority of the Christian community these characteristics become not only right but imperative. Notice two things: preaching and ministering—**whoever speaks . . . whoever renders service.** Communal worship—a community of service. How better can one describe the Christian fellowship in any age!

4:12-19. *A Further Admonition.* The purpose of the letter is now obvious: to encourage believers when trouble comes. Trouble is certain. Thus it must be met not with surprise but with glory to God. Actually, persecution can bring us into a more intimate fellowship with Christ in his sufferings. Suffering can not only bring **glory** to God; it can bring glory to the Christian.

The eschatological mood enters into this suffering: **When his glory is revealed, . . . the time has come.** It was an ancient idea that the people of God would be the first to suffer the judgment of God (verse 17; cf. Amos 3:2; Isaiah 10:12; Jeremiah 25:29; Ezekiel 9:6).

VI. CLOSING COUNSELS (5:1-14)

5:1-4. *A Message to Elders.* Elders had been officials in the synagogue. Here, however, the word refers to local officials in the Christian community whose function is the care of **the flock.** Paul had designated elders in the cities where he preached (Acts 14:23). While Peter as an apostle possessed an authority by virtue of his personal relation to Christ, here he identifies himself as **a fellow elder.** Such ministry entails the added role of suffering. Again, pastoral care is set in the context of pain—mutual pain within the community of faith.

Christ as **the chief Shepherd** directs the ministries of the undershepherds. Notice the repeated contrasts:

not by compulsion—but gladly;
not for **gain**—but with eager zeal;
not in lording it over the church—
but as an example in holy living.

5:5-11. *Final Exhortations.* Again note the contrasts: **humility** under God leads to victory (cf. "Whoever loses his life for my sake, he will save it," Luke 9:24). Undue anxiety is to be surrendered, since God is in charge (cf. Matthew 6:25-34). Be **sober** (clear-headed, cool) and alert since **the devil prowls** about **to devour** (cf. "Resist the devil and he will flee from you," James 4:7*b*).

5:10-11. Again the theme of suffering is used to show how it can be God's way of strengthening the believer. This is the painful price to be paid for the **glory** to come. Thus to God **be the dominion for ever and ever.**

5:12-14. *Conclusion.* Silvanus—Silas—apparently is the same person who helped Paul with I and II Thessalonians and who accompanied him on various journeys (Acts 15:40; 16:19, 25, 29; 17:4; 18:5). He was a prominent member of the church at Jerusalem (Acts 15:22, 27, 32) and was associated with Paul in preaching the gospel (II Corinthians 1:19).

5:13. Babylon doubtless refers to Rome, a title not intended to be complimentary (cf. Revelation 14:8). **Mark,** the John Mark of Acts 12:12, 25; 13:5, 13; 15:37, was the cousin of Barnabas. He is also mentioned in Colossians 4:10; II Timothy 4:11 and Philemon 24. Tradition has associated him with Peter, and the second gospel bears his name.

5:14. The **kiss of love,** practiced in the early church, has been replaced in our time by the handshake.

THE SECOND LETTER OF PETER

Claude Holmes Thompson

INTRODUCTION

This letter is concerned with vital issues for the Christian church. The author stoutly defends the orthodox faith of the apostolic community. Perhaps he has overstated this faith at one point—namely the parousia, or second coming of Christ. Likewise, he vigorously combats the threat of false teachers against the moral excellence of the Way (cf. Acts 9:2). Faith and life, doctrine and deportment—each is exceedingly important.

Authorship

While the letter bears the name of Simon Peter, hardly any scholar today—or even in the early church—regards it as having come from the apostle. Several reasons may be given for this judgment:

(1) Early Christian writers give scant reference to Peter as the author. This is in contrast to I Peter, which has good attestation.

(2) The author uses Jude, but Jude could hardly have been written early enough to have been known by Peter before his death.

(3) The criticism of the denial of Christ's second coming (3:1-4) suggests a late date. Nowhere else in the New Testament

are there any such denials. It is not likely that they arose before the destruction of the temple in A.D. 70, and Peter is thought to have died before this.

(4) There are clear differences between II Peter and I Peter in vocabulary, ideas, and use of the Old Testament. These differences were pointed out in the early church.

(5) The Hellenistic mood of the letter is not found in I Peter nor in the life of Peter which we see in the gospels and the sermons in Acts.

(6) The author refers to a collection of Paul's letters as "scriptures" (3:15-16). Certainly such a collection had not been made during Peter's lifetime.

But the letter itself claims to have come from Peter (1:1). What can we say of this? For one thing, the practice of writing under the name of another person was not uncommon in the ancient world. Jewish authors often wrote under the name of some revered person long dead. For example, we have documents supposedly written by Enoch, Moses, Ezra, Solomon, Daniel, Isaiah. Such writings were called "pseudonymous." This does not mean that they were false or forged. There are several such writings bearing the name of Peter—the Gospel of Peter, the Acts of Peter, the Apocalypse of Peter, and the Preaching of Peter. While these writings were known to the church in the second century, none of them won sufficient approval to be placed in the canon. We may never know why II Peter was so honored, but it was not simply because it bore the name of the apostle.

II Peter and Jude

No less than nineteen of the twenty-five verses of Jude are incorporated into or used in some manner by II Peter (II Peter 2:1–3:3). In addition there are other parallel ideas. Scholars substantially agree that II Peter used Jude rather than vice versa.

Date and Place of Composition

There seem to be several good reasons for dating this letter about the middle of the second century, or possibly as early as

125. Paul's letters had been collected and were regarded as "scripture" (3:15-16). The heretics who twisted Paul's letters "to their own destruction" (3:16) could have been followers of the heretic Marcion around A.D. 140. The apostles are clearly men of the past (3:2, 4). Finally, it was the middle or late second century before other writers explicitly referred to this letter at all. Perhaps this is as near as we can date II Peter, the last New Testament book to be accepted as scripture.

As for the place of composition, various suggestions have been made: Rome, Palestine, Asia Minor, Egypt. If the influence of I Peter is seen, perhaps this letter also came from Rome. But if Jude is from Palestine, as some believe, it is difficult to rule out this possibility.

Message

The author is disturbed over the threat to both the Christian ethic and doctrine by certain "lawless" men" (3:17). The faith is in jeopardy. The author is aware that the original leaders of the Christian movement are passing on. He feels a special urgency to call the church back to the purity of faith and practice that characterized its beginnings. Several elements are found in the message:

(1) The standard for Christian living is the witness of the prophets and apostles (1:19; 3:2).

(2) False teachers have arisen even within the fellowship (2:1). This was no casual matter. It threatened to destroy the very foundation of Christianity, even to the repudiation of Jesus himself.

(3) Central in this heresy was the denial of the return of Christ (3:3-7). Such a denial was essentially a denial of God's promise to complete his redemptive action begun in Christ.

(4) False teaching tended to result in false conduct (chapter 2). This ethical section of the letter is severe in its description of immorality.

(5) To bring about a new devotion to the faith two elements are necessary. First, attention should be given to Paul's letters, since these convey the authentic gospel (3:15-18). Second, a

true knowledge must replace false teaching (1:2-3, 5-6, 8, 20; 2:20-21; 3:3, 17-18).

With all the uncertainties surrounding this letter, it still brings an urgent call to devotion to the classic expression of the gospel. It is a clear voice in that period between the production of the major portions of the New Testament and the second century defenders of the faith, such as Justin Martyr, Irenaeus, and Tertullian.

I. LIFE AND GODLINESS (1:1-11)

1:1-2. *Salutation.* This is the only place in the New Testament, except in Acts 15:14, where Peter is given the name Simeon. Most often he is referred to as Peter, the name assigned to him by Jesus. The terms **servant** and **apostle** indicate that the author has been influenced by both I Peter and Jude.

1:1b. The **faith of equal standing with ours** designates the apostolic nature of that faith which rests not on human achievement but on **the righteousness of our God and Savior Jesus Christ.** This at once discredits the "false prophets" (2:1), claims the authority of the primitive Christians as the standard for the faith, and identifies the author with this standard.

1:2. Grace, as God's free forgiveness of sinners, brings **peace** as the assurance of divine favor. To these the author adds **knowledge.** This is not academic information, nor is it initiation into a mysterious religious experience. It is personal acquaintance with Jesus as Lord. The reference to Jesus as Lord is an echo of the earliest creed, or confession of faith—"Jesus is Lord" (cf. Romans 10:9; 14:9; I Corinthians 12:3; Philippians 2:11).

1:3-4. *Divine Provision for Human Need.* This true knowledge is the **divine power** which enables one to live the godly life. The source of this power is Jesus the Risen Lord. The godly life was concretely demonstrated in Jesus' earthly ministry. He was no mythical character created by an adoring church. **His own glory and excellence** are the pattern of the offer for us to **become partakers of the divine nature** (cf. John 17:3; Romans 5:2; II Corinthians 3:18).

1:4. It is no wonder that the author refers to this life as available through **his precious and very great promises.** Yet it is a promise, an offer, a gift which may be rejected. Received, it leads to full Christian faith and life.

1:5-11. *The Call for Response.* These verses contain what has been called "the ladder of virtues." They also show the consequences, pro and con, of our response to the divine promise. When one responds with faith, one receives the divine gift of new life. But this involves strenuous moral endeavor. Beginning with **faith** there is added a series of qualities of character: **virtue, . . . knowledge, . . . self-control, . . . steadfastness, . . . godliness, . . . brotherly affection, . . . love.** Cf. this list with the "fruit of the Spirit" named by Paul in Galatians 5:22-23.

II. Things to Remember (1:12-21)

1:12-21. *A Pastor's Concern.* The author is sure of two things. First, while the gospel is "good news," it is not "new news." Thus the witness is not to astonish his hearers with something they have never heard but **to remind** them **of these things** they already know. Second, they cannot learn the gospel so well as to be beyond danger of its loss. Thus they must be constantly reminded of God's grace.

1:14-15. There is a tenderness in the pastor's concern to establish his readers in the faith—since his own days are numbered. He compares his body with a tent (verse 14; see the Revised Standard Version footnote), as Paul does in II Corinthians 5:4. **The putting off of** his **body will be soon.** This common reference in the early church suggests the temporary nature of this life. The Christian attitude toward death is seen in the confidence that Jesus is Lord both of the present and the future.

1:16-21. *The Apostolic Witness.* Here the author contrasts the true gospel with the fables of the false teachers. He claims the authority of an eyewitness, assuming that his readers know the account of the transfiguration (Matthew 17:1-8; Mark 9:2-8; Luke 9:28-36). II Peter emphasizes the **majesty** of Jesus which was then revealed and which will again be seen at his return in glory. Thus when false teachers deny the second coming, they actually attack the majesty of Christ. This the author cannot tolerate.

Thus the gospel does not rest on fables, but on the validity of God's action in history, revealed in Jesus of Nazareth (verse 16). The transfiguration itself was a kind of foretaste of the second coming. As such it validated the apostolic witness on the plane of history, just as the prophetic faith had been declared within the framework of actual events on earth. The author also claims that this **prophetic word** points to the mission of Christ. Men are **to pay attention to this . . . until . . . the morning star rises in their hearts.**

1:20-21. These verses refer to the need for inspiration in interpreting the scriptures. Private opinions must be met by revelation of the Holy Spirit. The Bible is a book of the Christian community and must be interpreted within that community, the peculiar sphere where the Holy Spirit operates. In prophecy **men moved by the Holy Spirit spoke from God.** Thus the apostles as successors to the prophets were the special agents operating under the Spirit both to write and to interpret the scriptures. The same Spirit who inspired men of old to write also inspired persons within the church to understand the meaning. This is the protection against false teaching.

III. HINDRANCES TO THE FAITH (2:1–3:13)

2:1-3. *False Prophets—False Teachers.* This chapter should be studied in the light of Jude, especially 2:4-16, 18. Characteristics of false prophets and teachers are described. They work **secretly,** under cover. Their deception cannot bear the full light of the truth (cf. John 3:19-21). They promote destructive heresies—ideas of their own, private opinions which replace the judgment of the church. They deny **the Master who bought them** (cf. I Corinthians 7:23)—not by outright rejection, but by immoral influences upon the faithful. Their doom is sure, since they seduce others into sin and hence become victims of their own evil. **In their greed** they disguise the truth and bring the faith into disrepute.

2:4-11. *Judgment and Deliverance.* The author cites examples of God's judgments—**the angels** (Genesis 6:1-4), **the ancient world** (Genesis 6:5-7), **Sodom and Gomorrah** (Genesis 19:24-25). But he also shows how **Noah** (Genesis 6:8-22; 8:20-22) and **Lot** (Genesis 19:15-23) were rescued. Thus God saves the righteous in the midst of trouble while the wicked are condemned in terms of their own sins. Two evils are cited: **the lust of defiling passion** and the act of despising **authority.** The second describes those evil persons who live for only one world and disdain the realm of spiritual authority.

2:12-16. *The Evil That People Do.* This passage describes in detail the crass evil of the false teachers. The author, in brilliant defiance, scorns the immoral conduct which threatens the people of God.

2:12-14. Evil people are worse than brutes, since they disregard intelligence and hence live **like irrational animals.** But as the beasts are destined for capture and death, so destruction awaits these perverters of goodness. No longer do they seek the cover of darkness. They blatantly sin **in the daytime** and gloat in their persistent **adultery.** That is, they see in every woman the possibility of seduction. This is no occasional lapse. This is a calculated plan to express unbridled passion—and **entice unsteady souls.**

2:15-16. The author refers to the story of **Balaam,** who corrupted his prophetic office by covetousness and cowardice and hence turned Israel into sinful ways (Numbers 22–24). The irony of this old story is that the performance of the ass was more intelligent than the conduct of the prophet.

2:17-22. *When Freedom Becomes Bondage.* In the name of

emancipation there is a threat of new slavery. Paul warned against a false view of liberty turned into an occasion for indulgence (Galatians 5:13). This freedom is a freedom only to sin—with consequences of utter moral ruin. How can these false teachers **promise . . . freedom** when they themselves are **slaves of corruption?** The tragedy is that they once knew the way of the Lord but now have returned to **the defilements of the world.**

3:1-4. *Scoffers of Christ's Return.* A warning is raised against those who scoff at Christ's return. Both prophets and apostles had declared Christ to be the final judge and savior of all. But now, in the second or third generation of Christians, nothing had happened. Things remained pretty much the same **from the beginning of creation.** Thus, **"Where is the promise of his coming?"** This was obviously asked in scorn.

3:5-13. *The Scoffers Answered.* In an earlier age scoffers derided Noah. Still, the world was destroyed **by . . . water.** Created **out of water,** the earth is not impervious to ruin. This time the **destruction** will be by **fire.** This is the only New Testament reference to destruction of the earth by fire, but the idea is persistent in nonbiblical sources—Hebrew, Greek, and Roman. There is no built-in assurance of the claim that everything has remained the same since creation. If it was destroyed once, it will be destroyed again.

3:8-13. But again, God does not measure time by a clock or a calendar. The author uses Psalm 90:4 to help us see time as God sees it. God is in no hurry. God's delay is evidence of divine patience, since it is God's will **that all should reach repentance.** But God will act in time with sudden divine doom upon the wicked. Thus the Christian is to be engaged in watchful waiting, busy and eagerly desiring the day which will not be a terror but a joy. On verse 13 cf. Isaiah 65:17; 66:22; Romans 8:21; Revelation 21:1.

The idea of the second coming was deeply embedded in the life of the primitive church. Possibly some scholars have overemphasized the sense of immediate expectation shortly following Jesus' death. There is some question whether Jesus intended to leave an impression of such nearness, though some of his followers apparently did get this idea. Yet there seems little evidence that the church as a whole was confused by the nonreturn of Jesus. The fact that the author can describe this return as being **like a thief** suggests that neither the doctrine nor the delay greatly troubled the church.

IV. FINAL ADMONITIONS (3:14-18)

3:14-17. *A Call for Zeal.* The writer is convinced that the hope of Christ's return is needed to assure moral stability. In the meantime the task is to **wait** even as God waits. Even the divine patience, **the forbearance of our Lord,** is itself **salvation** in action. Judgment is delayed to provide opportunity for response. **Paul** is appealed to in support of this patience. Divine forbearance, however, must not encourage moral laxity. Thus these scoffers twist Paul's idea of freedom to promote license. While there may be things in Paul's letters **hard to understand**—perhaps in relation to freedom from the law—yet Paul may not be cited to promote immoral living.

3:15*b*-16. The reference to Paul's writings as scripture relates them to the Old Testament, **the other scriptures.** A collection of Paul's letters was probably known by around A.D. 90. Perhaps it is this collection to which the author refers.

3:17-18. *God's Gift of Grace.* Being forewarned by Paul's witness and by the author of II Peter, Christians can protect themselves against **the error of lawless men** and the loss of their **own stability**—that is, the inner foundation of a committed life. There is one security against this threat from without and within· **grow in the grace and knowledge of our Lord and Savior Jesus Christ.**

3:18*a*. Grace, that magnificently complex word, refers to the undeserved gift of God's love which can never be known or experienced save by the surrender of all trust in human skills and ability and the surrender to Jesus as Lord. **Knowledge** is instruction in the truth of the Christian tradition. Both grace and knowledge come from Christ. They characterize the growing Christian experience and life.

3:18*b*. The only proper response to such a lofty conception of Christian living is a doxology, here addressed directly to Christ (cf. Jude 25).

THE FIRST LETTER OF JOHN

Massey H. Shepherd, Jr.

INTRODUCTION

Form of the Letter

Since the later years of the second century I John has been
considered one of the catholic—that is general—letters of the New
Testament. Yet it lacks the customary address and greetings of a
letter. Hence many interpreters have described it as a sermon,
like the book of James, which has an introductory address but no
closing greetings. It has also been called a treatise, such as
Hebrews, which contains no opening address but has a doxology
and greetings at its close. Letter, sermon, or treatise—the writing
is addressed to a specific group of Christian believers. These
Christians may have belonged to one or to several congregations.
They include persons young and old, either in age or in their
Christian experience (cf. 2:12-14). They remain steadfast in the
"truth," in contrast to others who "went out" from the fellowship
that was "from the beginning" (cf. 2:18-27). Those who do hold to
the true testimony of God in Jesus Christ and remain in God's
communion are given exhortation and encouragement.

Authorship

Most students of the letter believe that the author is the same
person who wrote the gospel of John. The same style, the same

vocabulary, the same themes are in the two writings. Both documents appear to have been circulated and first cited at approximately the same time—the second quarter of the second century. They appeared in the same place—the Roman province of Asia (western Asia minor), whose capital was Ephesus. But the identity of this author has been much disputed. The preface of the letter (1:1-4) certainly links the author with the gospel, both its beginning (John 1:1-14) and its ending (John 20:19-29). Whether it presents the author as a personal eyewitness of Jesus or a disciple of one of the Lord's companions depends on the way one interprets the phrase "word of life" (see below on 1:1).

There are significant differences between the letter and the gospel. Stylistic differences are more apparent in the original Greek. But any reader can see that the letter is more abstract and less vivid and dramatic. It overworks certain constructions—for example, conditional sentences, antithetical sentences, sentences beginning with a demonstrative pronoun, and rhetorical questions.

The letter has none of the Semitic coloring of the gospel. Alone among writings of comparable length in the New Testament, it contains no quotation from the Old Testament. Maxims such as "God is light" (1:5) and "God is love" (4:8, 16) are peculiar. Other biblical books, including the gospel, employ more personal, less abstract ways of conveying "ideas" about the nature of God. On the other hand there are many expressions common to letter and gospel—for example, "born of God," "do the truth," "walk in darkness," overcome the world," and "keep the commandments."

The letter lacks certain fundamental keynotes of the gospel—the resurrection, the judgment, the kingdom; glory, grace, and peace. Some distinctive words and concepts in the letter are not found in the gospel—"fellowship," "anointing," "antichrist," and the description of Christ's redemptive work as an "expiation for our sins" (2:2, 4:10). A notable difference concerns the "advocate" (Paraclete). In the gospel he is the Holy

Spirit (John 14:16-17, 26; 15:26; 16:7). In the letter he is "Jesus Christ the righteous" (2:1).

All these contrasts of style and interest may be—and have been—explained. They are credited to the different form, purpose, and time of writing of the letter and the gospel. If indeed the gospel betrays indications (John 21:23-24) of having been edited by a "witness" of an earlier apostle or disciple of Jesus, it may be that this same person wrote I John. He may well be the "elder" who has left us the more personal and individual notes of II and III John (see comments). Some scholars believe that I John was written as an introduction to the gospel. Others believe it was composed some years after the gospel, by one whose advanced age shows signs of a weakening capacity for dramatic expression.

Date

The earliest citation of I John occurs in a letter of Bishop Polycarp of Smyrna to the church in Philippi. This letter was written shortly before 117. Eusebius of Caesarea, in his *Church History*, tells us that a contemporary of Polycarp, Bishop Papias of Hierapolis, also cited "testimonies" from the letter. In the last decade of the second century Irenaeus, bishop of Lyons and a pupil of Polycarp, credited the letter to the apostle John. So also did his contemporary Clement of Alexandria. But certain contemporaries of Irenaeus and Clement rejected all the Johannine writings as nonapostolic. They attributed them to one Cerinthus, a Jewish-Christian heretic who taught in Asia Minor in the early years of the second century.

No scholar today believes seriously that Cerinthus wrote the letter. On the contrary the letter, as also the gospel, is perhaps best understood as an answer to the teaching of Cerinthus. According to Irenaeus, Cerinthus was one of the first Gnostics. This philosophy taught that the world was made, not by the supreme God, but by an inferior power who was ignorant of the Father. Jesus was a man born as other humans. But because of his righteousness, prudence, and wisdom the heavenly "Christ" descended on him at his baptism, whereupon he proclaimed the "unknown Father" and performed miracles. But the Christ departed from him before the crucifixion and ascended back to the Father. Thus Cerinthus and other Gnostics distinguished between "Jesus" and "Christ." They denied the unity of his person in the incarnation, atonement, and resurrection.

Other early church writers tell us that Cerinthus was also a "Judaizer"—that is, he insisted on obedience to the Jewish law of circumcision and sabbath. He also favored the idea of a millennium of feasting and pleasure at the end of the present age when the righteous, including Jesus, would be raised from the dead. In the light of such teaching one appreciates the story told by Irenaeus. On encountering Cerinthus in the public baths at Ephesus, the apostle John exclaimed: "Let us flee, lest the bathhouse collapse, because Cerinthus the enemy of the truth is within!"

Teaching of the Letter

The author deals with the immediate, crucial issue of heresy. A broad background of boldly sketched strokes contrast the true nature of Christian faith and life over against error and sin. It is difficult to give a logical outline of his thought. Just as in the gospel, the letter throws out key words and phrases which recur again and again in similar but subtly altered contexts. The argument moves, not so much in a straight line as in a "spiral" of revolving, cumulative effects. The whole presentation is held together by the striking contrasts that come almost as synonyms: light, darkness, truth, lie; keeping the commandments, sin; love, hate; of the Father, of the world; him from the beginning, the evil one.

I. PREFACE (1:1-4)

The author's theme is the **word of life**—Jesus Christ. He is a truth about God, the ultimate reality. He is mediator of personal relationships that bring complete and perfect joy. He is himself a gospel—that is, "good news." He was a real person who was actually **heard** and **seen** and **touched** by others. He was also a revelation from God, with whom he shares eternally a life such as a father shares with a son. This same life he came to share with men and women.

The author associates himself with those who saw and heard him **from the beginning.** He hands on to his readers their testimony. The Christian gospel is both a message of truth and a **fellowship** of persons. It reconciles and unites God with humanity, and men and women with their fellows.

It is typical of the rich texture of language and thought in the Johannine writings that words and phrases suggest more than one meaning. Thus the **word of life** is also the Word of Life. It is not only a **that which,** a message of truth proclaimed, but a living person, who enters fully into our human community. Similarly the phrase **from the beginning** may refer to Christ's eternal existence with his Father, or it may point to the historical beginning of his appearing on earth.

This preface recalls, without actually quoting, the prologue of the gospel: "In the beginning was the Word. . . . In him was life. . . . And the Word became flesh and dwelt among us . . . ; we have beheld his glory." (John 1:1, 4, 14.) Likewise it reminds one of the resurrection scene when "he showed them his hands and his side" and "the disciples were glad when they saw the Lord" (John 20:20).

Hence it is not possible to tell with certainty whether the author was an actual eyewitness of Jesus or a believer in the testimony of eyewitnesses. In either case the fellowship with the Father and the Son is one and the same, unbroken and inseparable.

II. The Nature of Christianity (1:5–2:17)

1:5-10. *Fellowship with God.* The author's initial message would strike many chords in his readers: **God is light and in him is no darkness.** Ever since Plato, Greek philosophers used the imagery of light to describe the goodness and truth of ultimate reality. The religion of Zoroaster, stemming from Persia and increasingly influential in the Roman world, divided all reality into a mighty conflict of two opposing realms of light and darkness. The Gnostics made much of the idea. One of their earliest writings, The Gospel of Truth, says:

Ignorance of the Father has brought anguish and fear; and the anguish has become dense like a fog, so that none can see. . . . Through the mercies of the Father has been revealed the secret mystery, Jesus the Christ, through whom it has enlightened those who were in darkness because of forgetfulness. It (He) enlightened them and gave them a way. . . . As ignorance melts away when one gains knowledge, as darkness melts away when light appears, so incompleteness melts away in Completion."

No doubt the Gnostic author has in mind, as does the author of I John, the revealer of light, Jesus Christ, who is the light that "shines in the darkness, . . . the true light that enlightens every man . . . , the light of the world" (John 1:4, 9; 8:12).

But in the Johannine writings this light is not a merely abstract, principle of ultimate reality, of truth over against error and ignorance. It is a principle and guide of daily life that illumines personal relationships. It creates fellowship of humans with God and with one another. Light is the way of righteousness; sin is the way of darkness (cf. 2:8-11; John 3:19-21; 11:9-10). Light as a way of life is the Old Testament view, which the Johannine authors follow. It is to **walk** in the path of righteousness that God illumines.

2:1-6. *Fellowship with Christ.* The fundamental difference between Gnostic teaching and that of apostolic witness had to do with the nature of evil. For the Gnostics evil was simply error and ignorance, a misfortune for which one was not responsible. Christ came into the world to bring knowledge (*gnosis*) of the truth. Hence one needs only illumination, not forgiveness.

But the New Testament writers see the root of evil in **sin**—a deliberate rebellion against, and willful disobedience to, God's **commandments.** All people the **whole world** over are sinners.

To deny this fact is the real lie against truth. People need to be cleansed from sin, and this they cannot do for themselves. To say I **know him** and remain in sinful disobedience to God is a contradiction. How then does one extricate oneself from this dilemma?

Ancient peoples, whether Jew or pagan, conscious of sin and alienation from God, sought to do this by a sacrificial offering of **expiation.** This was usually a living—bloody—animal who was costly and hence in some degree a substitution for one's own life. But as Hebrews points out, such a manner of expiation—to "cover" or "blot out" sin and restore divine favor—was essentially ineffective. The victim was unwilling. The offerer in fact, if not in intention, was unrighteous. It is God who resolves our dilemma by sending a Son to be the **expiation for our sins** (cf. 4:10). Not only was the **blood of Jesus** (1:7) offered willingly. He was also, as offerer, perfectly righteous. He is our **advocate**, who pleads our cause and intercedes for us. Therefore by his act we may be assured that when we confess our sins God forgives us. But our confession is real only if we **keep his commandments** and **word.** We must abide in and **walk** in God's **way,** if our **love** and fellowship with God are to be **perfected.**

The Gnostics had no answer, despite their claim to superior knowledge. They ignored the fact of sin—for which they substituted mere ignorance. They also denied the reality of Christ's suffering and death. To them the "blood of Jesus" had no significance, since they separated the human Jesus from the divine Christ.

2:7-17. *Fellowship with the Church.* The author always insists that theological truth can never be separated from ethical demand. If we accept God's forgiving love for Christ's sake, we must love one another as God loved us. The **commandment** of love is the summary and fulfillment of all commandments—**from the beginning.** Yet Jesus gave it a new form: "This is my commandment, that you love one another as I have loved you" (John 15:12). By the fruits of love one may know whether one is in **light** or in **darkness.** Love for one's **brother** and neighbor, not theoretical knowledge, is the only true test of Christian discipleship. It embraces all people of all ages—children, the young and the old.

Love is not the principle of life in the **world.** In the Johannine writings the term "world" does not mean, as with the Gnostics, the material creation of God. It refers to those who are alienated from God by setting their ultimate values on the **things in the world** and following the tempting example of the **evil one.** Cerinthus, for example, stressed the coming millennium as a time devoted to sensual pleasures (see Introduction). Darkness has blinded the eyes of such persons. They do not realize that Christ in his temptation conquered the world, the flesh, and the devil—the selfish **lust** and **pride** of self-centered existence. Nor do they see that Christ is at work now in the world, as ever new disciples **overcome the evil one.** Thereby a process is taking place by which **the darkness is passing away and the true light is already shining.**

III. THE CRISIS OF CHRISTIANITY (2:18–4:6)

2:18-27. *The Coming of Antichrist.* Jesus viewed his coming into the world as a prelude of the final crisis of history—**the last hour**—the inauguration of the kingdom of God. In this crisis the forces of evil would marshall all their powers in an attempt to defeat God. They would trouble and deceive his righteous ones—through wars, tumults, and persecutions, schisms and divisions, and "false Christs and false prophets" (Mark 13:22) who perform wondrous miracles. In the Synoptic gospels these signs are presented in apocalyptic form (cf. Mark 13; Matthew 24; Luke 21:5-36; see Introduction to Revelation). In Revelation 12-13 they are symbolized in the monster figures of the dragon (Satan) and his blasphemous beast who would usurp the worship of Christ the Lamb. The same crisis is predicted in the gospel of John—for example, 15:20–16:11—though in less flamboyant imagery. Its whole message is pervaded by Jesus' pronouncements of a coming "hour" which will be decisive.

Quite likely the author of I John invented the symbol of

antichrist as a sign of this **last hour.** He sees its appearance first of all in the schism produced in the church by the teaching of a false Christ. This would have been the doctrine that Jesus and the Christ are not one and the same **Son** of the **Father.** Therefore Jesus Christ did not "come in the flesh" (cf. 4:2-3; II John 7). Presumably the early Gnostic groups who taught this doctrine **went out** of the church voluntarily. But the elder in II John 10 advises a more positive policy of excluding them.

In verse 27 the author makes an interesting play on the word **anointing.** *Christos* is the Greek equivalent of the Hebrew word transliterated Messiah, the "Anointed One." In the Old Testament kings, priests, and prophets were consecrated in their office by a ceremony of anointing. So the true Messiah, Jesus Christ, fulfills these roles by his anointing with the Holy Spirit (cf. Acts 10:38). Those who abide in him have received his anointing and become in him a "royal priesthood" (I Peter 2:9). Thus they are all initiated into his truth and need no further teaching.

The Gnostics with their superior knowledge of the heavenly *Christos* made much of this anointing. They claimed that it imparted their more advanced truth. It was linked with the "chrism" or oil used in the ceremonial anointing of initiates immediately following their baptism in water. One of the Gnostic writings, the Gospel of Truth, speaks of how Christ "will anoint them with the ointment. The anointing is the mercy of the Father who will have mercy on them. But those whom he has anointed are perfect."

2:28–3:12. *Children of God and of the Devil.* The separation of the true **children of God** from those of the **world** is also a sign of the last hour. The difference will be clearly seen at Christ's second coming. The righteous will be revealed like him—pure, loving, obedient in keeping God's commandments. This is their confidence and their hope.

The gospel of John uses bold metaphors of begetting and birth, both of Christ's intimate relation with God the Father and of the believer's with the Father and the Son (cf. John 1:12-13, 18; 3:3-16). These figures were much exploited by the Gnostics.

117

In their interpretation "seeds" of the divine Being were scattered among people in this world. Christ came to collect and return them to God by way of his revealing knowledge. A person's moral condition and behavior had nothing to do with this predestined return of the seed to its divine source.

The author uses language as astonishing as that of his opponents: **No one born of God commits sins; for God's nature,** literally "seed," **abides in him.** But he controls his statement by the context. He does not mean to say that the the the new birth demanded by Jesus produces a person who is sinless (cf. 1:10). Rather, one who is born of God is set in the right direction—of doing what is right and loving their neighbors. Sin is a matter not of nature but of conduct. Love is the test of those who are truly born of God. Cf. I Peter 1:23, which in turn probably goes back to the interpretation of the parable of the weeds (Matthew 13:37-38).

3:13-24. *Persecution.* Jesus predicted that the **world** would hate his disciples, as it hated him, even to death (John 15:18–16:4). Out of hatred comes the impulse to kill. Indeed Jesus equated hatred with murder (Matthew 5:21-22, 43-45). He warned his disciples strictly against the temptation to strike back. Love knows no enemies, and least of all any person in need.

When I John was written, persecution of Christians by the Roman state was already a constant menace, even though it was not persistently pursued. In Asia Minor it appears to have been especially grievous for the decade of the 90's. We know this both from I Peter and Revelation and from the correspondence of Pliny, the Roman governor of Bithynia, with the Emperor Trajan in 112. It is ironic that the Roman historian Tacitus (55-120) should sum up the opinion which the pagan populace had of Christianity as "hatred of the human race." (Annals xv.44.5). The Christian's only consolation in suffering was the assurance that Christ's example was being followed, and the confidence of a good conscience before God. Cf. I Peter 2:21-25; 4:12-19.

4:1-6. *Contradiction of Prophetic Spirits.* In the apostolic age prophecy was considered one of the highest gifts of the Spirit of God to the church. Yet even Paul, who held this gift in utmost esteem, realized that not all **spirits** spoke the truth (cf. I Corinthians 12:3 and II Corinthians 11:4). Jesus warned his disciples about **false prophets** (Matthew 7:15). He predicted their appearance, with their deceiving signs and teachings, as indicative of the last times (Matthew 24:11, 24; Mark 13:22). The testing of prophets was no light matter, however. It might be a presumptuous testing of God. This passage offers two basic criteria for the test:

(1) doctrine, especially the prophet's teaching about the nature and person of Jesus;

(2) manner of life, whether the prophet is **of the world.**

IV. THE VICTORY OF CHRISTIANITY (4:7–5:17)

4:7–5:3. *In Perfect Love.* In the preceding sections the author has developed his themes with reference to the statement "God is light." He has said repeatedly that the truth of God and knowledge of God cannot be separated from the character of daily living in obedience to God's righteous commandments. Now in conclusion he turns the same arguments around, with reference to the statement **God is love.** All he has said about truth is now said about love. Christian belief and Christian life are inseparably linked. As one believes, so one lives. As one lives, so is one's real belief.

The initiative is always from God. God loved first. God sent a Son to expiate our sins, to be our Savior. God has given us the Spirit. So if we believe in him, confess him, and show our love for him by loving our neighbors, we may confidently face the coming **judgment** without **fear.** To live in love is to live victoriously over all error and all anxiety.

5:4-12. *In the True Faith.* The Christian overcomes the external punishment of the world and the internal fear of the heart by love. The falsehoods, lies, and disbelief of the world, and any inner doubts are overcome by **faith.** It is remarkable that only here (verse 4) in the Johannine writings do we find the word **faith** so common in all the other New Testament documents. It has therefore a climactic force. But though the noun "faith" is rare in Johannine usage, the related verb "believe,"—"have faith"—runs through all the writing. It appears in every nuance of grammatical construction, and especially in this passage:

(1) Believe God (verse 10, verb with dative)—accept God's word, trust God to be credible.

(2) Believe in God's witness concerning the Son (verse 10, verb with preposition)—live in full confidence and reliance on God's revelation.

(3) Believe that . . . (verse 5, verb with subordinate clause)—acknowledge as true what God reveals.

Thus the Johannine writers have a much deeper insight into faith than the Gnostics. Christianity is much more than a system of belief and knowledge of a revealed doctrine—though this is important too. Christianity is right belief about God's revelation in Christ. Christian faith reaches down to the very basis and ground of life—our deepest convictions about God's relation to us and to the world. It shapes the way these convictions show our trust, and witness to this trust, in the everyday issues of our life.

Faith is grounded in the **witness** of God, first of all. We can only proclaim what we have seen and heard from God (cf. 1:2; John 3:31-36). And God's witness is the whole life and death of the incarnate Jesus Christ. His birth, his baptism, his ministry, his perfect obedience, his bloody death, his resurrection were all wrought by the power of God's Spirit. Without the witness of that Spirit—the Spirit of **truth**—his baptism in **water** and his death in **blood** (cf. John 19:34) would be only that of an ordinary person, not of the Son of God, in whom and by whom we have **eternal life.**

The **three witnesses** of verse 8—**the Spirit, the water, and the blood**—may be an allusion to the church's sacramental rites of initiation. These were confirmation, baptism, and Eucharist, in the form and order observed in the churches of Asia Minor at the time of writing of I John. During the controversies of the fourth century over the doctrine of the Trinity the text was expanded by the insertion: "There are three that bear record in heaven, the Father, the Word, and the Holy Spirit: and these three are one." A few late Greek manuscripts contain the addition. Hence it passed into the King James Version. But all modern critical editions and translations of the New Testament, including the Revised Standard Version, omit this insertion. It has no warrant in the best and most ancient manuscripts or in the early church fathers.

5:13-21. *In Answer to Prayer.* "Whatever you ask in my name, I will do it" (John 14:13-14). So Jesus promised his disciples. To pray in his **name,** to pray as he prayed, is to offer perfect prayer, for it is prayer that is always according to God's will. Such prayer is always answered—though the answer may be different from our expectations. This assurance that God **hears** and answers our prayer is for Christians the final confidence in victory. They know they are guarded by God, and no power of sin or of the devil can ultimately claim them.

There is a disturbing note in this final summation of the author, however—the suggestion that there is an evil, a **mortal sin,** over which no prayer can prevail. It is possible that the author has in mind the Gnostics, who repudiated the fact of sin and consequently felt no need for repentance and forgiveness. But more probably he includes Gnostics within a larger category of all who deliberately commit apostasy.

Jesus gave solemn warning of the fateful judgment of those who openly denied him (Matthew 10:32-33; Mark 8:38; Luke 9:26; 12:8-9). And another tradition of the sayings recorded the unpardonable sin of blasphemy—the lie given to God's Spirit by attributing his work to Satan (Matthew 12:31-32; Mark 3:28-29; Luke 12:10). Such a lie is indeed the antichrist (cf. 2:22)—a mortal sin that goes beyond all will and capacity to distinguish right from wrong.

The early church was most severe in its judgment on the deliberate apostasy by any of its members (cf. Hebrews 6:4-6; 12:16-17). It offered no hope of reconciliation. There can be no accommodation between worship of the one true God and any other substitute for God, which is idolatry. Hence the final warning of the letter: **keep yourselves from idols.**

THE SECOND LETTER OF JOHN

Massey H. Shepherd, Jr.

AUTHORSHIP

II John is a specific illustration and application of the concerns of I John. The similarity of thought and expression in the two letters makes it obvious they were written by the same person.

Who then is the **elder** of verse 1? The word in Greek, as in English, means literally an "old man." In Jewish communities from ancient times a council of elders supervised the administration and interpretation of the law. In New Testament times these councils were no doubt modeled on the great council in Jerusalem—the Sanhedrin—with its "chief priests, scribes, and elders." At the synagogue assemblies the elders were given seats of honor.

The church in apostolic times took over the institution. The apostles and elders of the church in Jerusalem served as model for the elders of local Christian communities (cf. Acts 14:23; 20:17). The term was broad enough to include all leaders who exercised oversight and pastoral care in the congregations (cf. I Peter 5:1; James 5:14; Titus 1:5-6). Here the elder speaks with authority—in the singular, not as a member of a council group. But his personal identity and rank and the basis of his authority are not clear.

THE ADDRESS

The letter is a message from one Christian congregation to another, either in Ephesus or in the province of Asia (see Introduction to I John). The gracious figure used to describe the two churches in this exchange—**the elect lady and her children** (verse 1), **the children of your elect sister** (verse 13)—has a parallel in I Peter 5:13, which was also written by an apostle-elder.

Elect indicates those who are especially "chosen" of God. The figure of the church as a **lady** derives from the bridegroom-bride, husband-wife imagery common in the Old Testament to express the loving relation of God to Israel. In the New Testament it expresses Christ's love for his church (cf. Matthew 9:15; 25:1-13; II Corinthians 11:2; Ephesians 5:23-25; John 3:29; Revelation 21:2, 9).

THE SITUATION

The themes of **truth** and **love** are the bases of the elder's warning to the **lady**—that is, the congregation meeting in the **house** (verse 10). At this period the churches met in private homes offered in hospitality to Christians for their instruction and worship. They were often instructed by wandering prophets and teachers, visiting preachers and lecturers. But by the latter years of the first century many of these visitors were **deceivers** (verse 7). The elder is concerned lest the Christian virtue of hospitality be used as a cover for these false teachers.

He has in mind the same heretics who are combated in I John—the early Gnostics (see Introduction to I John). They claim to have a more advanced teaching than what has been handed down **from the beginning** (verse 5), especially suited for one who **goes ahead** of other Christians (verse 9). Thus they divide the fellowship, not following the **commandment** to **love one another** (verse 5). Their doctrine is nothing less than a sign of Satan—**the deceiver and the antichrist** (verse 7). For they do not acknowledge that the Christ, the Son of the Father, was truly incarnated in the humanity of Jesus. By their false division of the man Jesus and the divine Christ these heretics split every fellowship and every communion, by which the Father **abides in** the Son, and Jesus Christ the Son **abides in** his Father and in us, and we **abide in** him and in one another.

THE THIRD LETTER OF JOHN

Massey H. Shepherd, Jr.

AUTHORSHIP AND ADDRESS

In contrast to II John (see comment) this letter of the **elder** is personal, not an exchange between churches. Its recipient is **Gaius**—a common name in the Roman world. He is otherwise unknown, as are also the other persons named in the letter. Nor is it at all certain that the church congregations of the two letters are the same. In both letters the elder writes briefly—and for us today somewhat cryptically—in view of an impending visit and meeting **face to face** (verse 14). Personal interviews are more effective than **pen and ink** in resolving problems of broken relationships and misunderstandings.

THE SITUATION

It is tempting to see the situation in Gaius' church as comparable to that of the congregation addressed in II John. The elder takes pains to stress the **truth** which Gaius follows and the **love** which he practices. In both letters the question of Christian hospitality is raised.

Yet in fact the situation indicated in the two letters seems to be reversed. In II John, the elder warns the church not to give hospitality to false teachers. But in this letter the elder's friends, who have received hospitality from Gaius, have been rejected and put out of the church by one **Diotrephes** (verse 9). Presumably Diotrephes is a local church authority. What position **Demetrius** (verse 12) holds is not clear. He may be the leader of the visiting Christians whom Diotrephes has refused to **welcome.**

It should be noted that the elder accuses Diotrephes, not of false teaching and heresy, but of resistance to the elder's authority. It is possible of course that their differences are doctrinal. But some interpreters think not. They see in Diotrephes an emerging leader—perhaps bishop—of a local church who is concerned to keep his church free from outside interference. It often happens that younger leaders in the churches find difficult, and at last unbearable, the dictatorial ways of older persons who set themselves up as authorities— even with the best of intentions and out of considerable experience.

Hospitality may also become burdensome by repeated and unnecessary visits of **strangers.** But throughout the New Testament it is stressed as a primary virtue of Christian love (cf. Matthew 10:40-42; 25:34-40; Romans 12:13; Hebrews 13:2; I Peter 4:9).

THE BOOK OF JUDE

Claude Holmes Thompson

INTRODUCTION

See the Introduction to II Peter for the relationship between that letter and Jude. The fiery denunciations of Jude were used in II Peter in an attack upon the enemies of the faith (cf. verses 4-16, 18 with II Peter 2). Thus the two writings have much in common as they face a dual threat to the church. The first was antinomianism (see below on verse 4). The second was some form of Gnosticism, a heresy within the early Christian church which claimed to have special knowledge (*gnosis*) concerning salvation and which considered all matter evil. The latter view led either to asceticism on the one hand or to complete moral license on the other.

Author and Date

The author calls himself Jude (Judas), the "brother of James," who apparently is to be identified as the "brother of the Lord." But this close relationship with Jesus is doubtful. "The faith which was once for all delivered to the saints" (verse 3) seems to be a second century expression. The era of the apostles is apparently well in the past (verse 17). The letter condemns the Gnostic heresies which arose late in the first century.

Most scholars feel it was written in the second century, hence not by Jude the brother of Jesus. But the question has been raised as to why a writer would have used the name of such an undistinguished and almost unknown brother of the Lord. Apparently the purpose was to establish his message as in harmony with the apostolic gospel—which he sought to defend.

A "General" Epistle

From about the fourth century seven letters of the New Testament have been known as "general" or "catholic" epistles—James and I, II Peter and I, II, and III John; and Jude. Although II and III John are specifically directed to persons, all seven have borne this title, meaning that they have been addressed to the whole Christian community. Jude simply says, "To those who are called"—about as general a designation as could be found. It has been suggested, however, that perhaps this letter was written to Jewish Christians, since there are repeated references to the Old Testament and other Jewish writings (verses 9-15). Yet the evils portrayed suggest the sexual irregularities which Paul met in Gentile communities (cf. I Corinthians 6:12; Galatians 5:13). It is possible that the readers were Jews of the Dispersion who knew both cultures. As for the place of composition, it is unknown.

Message

The book was produced in a crisis. It was written to defend the Christian faith against ungodly persons who threatened it by corrupt doctrine and practices.

I. Introduction (Verses 1-4)

Verses 1-2. *Salutation.* **A servant of Jesus Christ**—literally "slave"—was not an uncommon designation of an author (cf. Romans 1:1; Philippians 1:1; James 1:1; II Peter 1:1). It suggests a special devotion to Jesus as Lord. In the words **called, beloved,** and **kept** note the strength of the believer's relation to

God. Those who respond are kept through love for Christ, perhaps implying a security until the final judgment.

Verses 3-4. *The Reason for the Letter.* A threat had developed which endangered the Christian movement. Thus the author proceeds to defend **the faith.** This faith was not restricted to saving faith, as in Paul (cf. Romans 3:21-31). Nor was it mere trust in God's protection (cf. Matthew 6:25-34). It was not even an assurance of a blessed future (cf. Hebrews 11:1). The faith now had become clearly defined doctrine as well as a way of life.

The author starts to write concerning the **common salvation**—that is, the salvation belonging to all Christians. But a vigorous defense of the faith becomes of immediate concern. Believers are the custodians of the faith given **once for all.** The fact that the author simply refers to this faith is evidence that it was well known and carefully defined. While it was not a fully developed system of theology, it did set forth God's redemptive action in Christ as the beginning of salvation. This salvation was not a human achievement; it was divine action. This message is found at every level of New Testament witness.

Verse 4. The emergency is urgent since **ungodly persons** have become part of the community of faith. They not only deny Jesus Christ as Lord. They even exploit his gracious love as an opportunity for immorality. The danger from this evil was that it was within the church. While their ultimate doom was sure, something had to be done about these persons lest the whole community be contaminated (cf. I Corinthians 5). Such evil could not be harbored within the fellowship.

Apparently the evil here is a form of antinomianism. This is the teaching that a person living within the faith is free from observing the law. This perversity has a long history. Paul met it (cf. Romans 3:8; 6:1, 15). It erupted within the Reformation in the sixteenth century. Some early Methodists claimed to be above the necessity of keeping the moral codes, only to be positively repudiated by John Wesley. It has again become known in our time under the popular idea of "once saved, always saved," or the dangerous teaching of the eternal security of believers.

II. THE HERETICS AND THEIR PUNISHMENT (VERSES 5-16)

Verses 5-7. *God's Punishment of Sinners.* The idea that God is too nice to punish evildoers would have been utterly unacceptable to the author of Jude. Just as the church received the perpetually valid faith, so it also learned **once for all** of God's judgment. Examples are given to show that God takes an active role in the punishment of sinners. Unbelievers in Israel en route from **Egypt** to Canaan, the unfaithful **angels** in heaven, **Sodom and Gomorrah**—all experienced divine rejection. The unbelief of Israel fares no better than the lustful immorality of the Sodomites (cf. Numbers 13–14). Even the ambitious angels in heaven were put into **eternal chains in the nether gloom until the judgment of the great day.** The reference comes from the nonbiblical book of Enoch. The fate of Sodom and Gomorrah was well known. It is used extensively to illustrate divine judgment. The warning here is of alarming urgency, since it illustrates God's severe judgment upon those who turned from a privileged position in faith.

Verses 8-10. *Sin Unmasked.* Three manifestations of evil are particularly repugnant to the author—defilement of **the flesh,** rejection of **authority,** and scorn of **the glorious ones.** These evils are the result of what is called **dreamings,** a sort of reverie in fantasy. This likely refers to claims of special revelation or inspiration which releases one from the normal demands of common decency. Hence the Gnostics and antinomians felt that since the flesh is evil, what one does with it has no moral significance. Thus the instincts of the body may be given full license. Likewise, since God's grace covers everything, sin is merely the occasion for a fuller expression of divine mercy. No wonder authority is rejected. It interferes with unchecked sexual indulgences.

Verses 8-9. Scorn of the **glorious ones,** is a bit obscure. Possibly it indicates mockery of the divine glory to which a multitude of angels bore witness. A vivid illustration is given from a Jewish writing, the Assumption of Moses, where **the archangel Michael** does not even rebuke **the devil** as he greedily seeks **the body of Moses.** Only God is adequate for such judgment. Yet these false leaders of Jude's day presume to act even against God.

Verses 11-13. *Unrelieved Doom.* Three examples of severe judgment are now cited:

(1) **Cain** (Genesis 4:3-16) is more than a murderer. He typifies the man who exists in a living judgment of self-seeking, greed, and treachery. He is always running away—from everything except himself.

(2) **Balaam** (Numbers 22-24) is the covetous false prophet who taught Israel to sin.

(3) **Korah** (Numbers 16) resisted the divinely appointed authority of Moses so needed for consolidation of the nation. Basically all three are examples of the danger which the author of Jude saw in rejecting God's way and the indulging in self-seeking.

Verses 12-13. A series of vivid metaphors pictures the fate of these perverse souls:

(1) **Blemishes,** blots **on your love feasts**—They selfishly consume the food provided at their love feasts with no thought for its sacramental significance. Hence they make holy observances into times of revelry (cf. I Corinthians 11:20-34). This sort of conduct destroyed the very idea of Christian love in the feast.

(2) **Waterless clouds, carried along by winds,** mock the parched fields. The erring ones have become impostors, useless and empty.

(3) They are like **fruitless trees in late autumn, twice dead, uprooted.** At the time of harvest they merely clutter the ground.

(4) Like **wild waves of the sea,** they cast **up the foam of their own shame**—mere bubbly froth which does not even make a noise when it disintegrates.

(5) They may desire to shine as **stars** in the heavens. But they become flaming meteors burning themselves away to nothingness.

Verses 14-16. *Judgment Foreseen.* The author quotes from the book of Enoch to show that this form of godlessness had been foreseen in the distant past. He erroneously attributes the book to **Enoch in the seventh generation from Adam,** but it actually appers to have been written in the first century B.C. So serious is the evil that God alone is able to manage the situation. Hence God sends **his holy myriads** in judgment.

Verse 16. Three final characteristics of these false leaders are described:

(1) They are **grumblers,** full of surly discontent.

(2) They are **malcontents,** complaining that their lot in life is unfair. They want to express **their own passions** to escape their drab existence.

(3) **As loud-mouthed boasters,** they arrogantly flout their own importance. They flatter other people only to exploit them.

III. THE FOUNDATION OF FAITH (VERSES 17-23)

Verses 17-19. *The Witness of the Apostles.* The actual source of the quotation referring to **scoffers** and those who follow **their own ungodly passions** has not been found in apostolic documents. But research into the "twilight period" (A.D. 30–60) of the oral tradition discloses an element of apprehension of danger to the faith. This oral tradition was part of the preaching of the church before the New Testament was written.

Verses 20-23. *The Basis of Positive Goodness.* Goodness can never be merely negative. However skillful one may be in refuting evil, more than this is required. Again the basis is the author's insistence upon the faith, **your most holy faith.** That faith is a divinely given deposit, the only foundation for Christian living. Faith and practice, theology and life, doctrine and conduct are inseparable.

Verses 20-21. But this faith is no static thing. There must be progress, development, even in its practice. Specific directions are given for:

(1) Prayer. Life in which **the Holy Spirit** resides is the true pattern of Christian living, and prayer is inspired by the Holy Spirit (cf. Romans 8:26).

(2) Active obedience. The gift of **the love of God** is a divine activity. But without the corresponding human response in devoted obedience, this gift will be lost.

(3) Patient expectation. Since the faith is **unto eternal life,** the present distress requires the long look and the hope that even evildoers may be brought to repentance.

Verses 22-23. In an epistle of such fierce denunciations against evil it is healthy to find judgment relieved by hope. Perhaps the false leaders may be saved. Clear reasoning has its place. Doubters are to be confronted by intelligent persuasion. Others must be rescued from the very brink of ruin. But it is likely that some are beyond redemption. And while compassion must always be a Christian virtue, it still includes **hating even the garment spotted by the flesh.**

IV. THE BENEDICTION (VERSES 24-25)

Verse 24. *Aid from God.* After all the trouble described in this brief letter, this moving benediction is like a breath of fresh air. Though one may live in the midst of sin, God **is able to keep you from falling.** This is no temporary aid. It will be sustained until we stand **before the presence of his glory.**

Verse 25. *Salvation Through Christ.* Salvation is regarded as God's gift, but the bestowal of the gift is accomplished **through Jesus Christ.** The church accordingly confesses and obeys him as **Lord,** since he alone effectively acts for God.

THE REVELATION TO JOHN

S. MacLean Gilmour

INTRODUCTION

Apocalyptic Literature

The opening words of the Revelation were probably its
original title: "The revelation of Jesus Christ, which God gave
him . . ." "Revelation" translates a Greek word that is
transliterated "apocalypse." Though so far as we know
Revelation was the earliest writing to use this word as a title,
apocalyptic, or "revealed," literature had long been familiar to
both Jews and Christians.

Even at early levels in its development nearly every religion
has some eschatology—a doctrine of last things—that leans in
the direction of apocalyptic ideas. There are passages in Amos,
Micah, Isaiah, and Jeremiah which prepared the way for the
later Jewish apocalyptists—especially those passages in which
the prophets reflected popular speculation about the coming
"day of Yahweh." This apocalyptic tendency in the literature of
the Old Testament was heightened after the Babylonian exile.
The imagery and symbolism of Ezekiel, Joel, Isaiah 24–27, and
Zechariah 9–14 are apocalyptic in character. They prepared the
way for the book of Daniel, the first full-blown apocalypse.

Jewish apocalyptic had its roots, then, in Old Testament
prophecy. But its development was the result of alien influence.

Babylonian and Persian literature reveals at an earlier date than does the Old Testament the chief apocalyptic traits:

(1) a pronounced dualism in the doctrine of the two ages,

(2) the ideas of a resurrection and a final judgment,

(3) descriptions of the catastrophic events that will mark the end of the present age and inaugurate the new.

It is no accident that apocalyptic ideas became established within Judaism after the exile, for the Jews were then vassals of the Persians. It was almost inevitable that a view of history which dominated the thought of Judaism's powerful overlord should leave its mark on postexilic Jewish writing.

The earliest and most influential of the extant Jewish apocalypses is Daniel. It was written in 165-164 B.C. during the Maccabean revolt against Antiochus Epiphanes of Syria. Apocalyptic literature flourished in Judaism for the next century and a half, until the destruction of Jerusalem by the Romans in A.D. 70 and for a time thereafter. Among the scores of Jewish apocalyptic books that are known in whole or in part are the various writings ascribed to Enoch (notably I Enoch), the Testaments of the Twelve Patriarchs, the Jewish Sibylline Oracles, the Ascension of Moses, the central section of II Esdras (chapters 3–14), often known as IV Ezra, the Apocalypse of Baruch, and the "War Scroll" found among the Dead Sea Scrolls.

Apocalyptic literature reflects the historical situation at the time of writing. The various apocalyptic books were tracts of their times—one might even say tracts for bad times. There was a general framework of ideas. Details differed according to the interest and emphasis of the individual author. In some writings the chief interest lay in the extraordinary events that would herald the end of the present age. In others it was religious: How would God vindicate justice? In some the Messiah was the central figure. In others he was not even mentioned. In some God's kingdom would be established on this earth. In others God would reign in a re-created heaven and earth. In some all Jews would be raised from the dead at the end of the present age and would inherit the new age of God's rule. In others only a remnant would share in the good time coming. In still others the redeemed would consist only of those Jews who would be alive at the last day.

With all its variety and flexibility Jewish apocalyptic literature shared a number of leading ideas:

(1) Time is divided into two ages. The present age is evil. It is dominated by Satan's demonic hosts. But the coming age is at hand, the age in which God alone will reign. Satan and his demonic powers will be destroyed, and their allies on earth will perish. The elect in Israel will enjoy prosperity and peace on a transformed earth or in a new heaven and a new earth.

(2) The end of the present age is to come with dramatic suddenness. God will intervene suddenly and catastrophically in the processes of history and God's purposes will be accomplished.

(3) The end is expected almost immediately. It is not a far-off divine event toward which creation is moving but a consummation that is anticipated in the immediate future. The author of Daniel and many of his successors make various estimates of the time of the end that have fascinated innumerable readers to this day. But in no case do they think of the end as more than a few months or a few years distant.

(4) The end of the present evil age is to be marked by a period of extreme distress. "The woes of the Messiah" is a term occasionally used to describe the events of this premessianic tribulation. Natural catastrophes, a breakup of the cosmic order, plagues, famines, wars—such are the horrors on which the authors love to dwell. The idea behind such speculation is that the worst will have to come before God can intervene. But apocalyptic writers always believe that they live in the last days. The end is at hand!

Christian Apocalypses

The extent to which Jesus was influenced by apocalyptic thought is still a matter of debate. It would appear that he took over many apocalyptic ideas of his day and age. At the same time he interpreted the apocalyptic scheme in such a way that his thought became virtually independent of it.

For example, the apocalyptic doctrine of the two ages was basic to his teaching about the kingdom of God. But the gospels indicate that he modified it in a radical fashion. The full accomplishment of God's rule belonged to the future. Only then would the kingdom "come with power." In his own ministry, however, the end time was already manifesting itself on earth. The new age of God's rule had already broken in on history before the old age had completely run its course. The kingdom of God was more than a hope. It was a new order already being realized.

However we may understand Jesus' thought of the future, it is clear that the early church lived in an atmosphere of apocalyptic expectation. Early Christians thought in terms of the imminent return of Christ as the vicegerent of God. They expected that the new age of God's rule would be inaugurated in dramatic fashion with that return. Believers, Paul declared, were those who had "turned to God from idols, to serve a living and true God, and to wait for his Son from heaven" (I Thessalonians 1:9-10).

Parts of the New Testament that conform to the apocalyptic scheme include:

> Mark 13 (and its parallels in Matthew and Luke)
> I Corinthians 15:20-28
> II Corinthians 5:1-3
> I Thessalonians 4:15-17
> II Thessalonians 2:1-12
> Hebrews 12:22-23

Christians early took over many Jewish apocalypses and edited and adapted them—for example, IV Ezra, the Testaments of the Twelve Patriarchs, and the Ascension of Isaiah. Early in the second century such Christian apocalypses were written as the Apocalypse of Peter and the Shepherd of Hermas. But the first and most important of the specifically Christian apocalypses is Revelation.

Apocalyptic Differences in Revelation

One feature of Jewish apocalypses is their pseudonymity. They claim to have been written by some great figure of a remote era—Daniel, Ezra, Moses, Enoch, Noah. The fact that the book has remained unknown for so long is often accounted for by the statement that the author was ordered to hide or "seal" his revelation until the last days. The assumption is that it has been "found" when the times to which the revelation applies have at last come.

Revelation is not a pseudonymous book. Its author writes under his own name: "I John [of Patmos], your brother, who shares with you in Jesus the tribulation and the kingdom and the patient endurance" (Revelation 1:9). His message is the "revelation of Jesus Christ" and is imparted under his own authority.

Claiming to be the work of ancient seers, Jewish apocalypses also claim to be visions of the future set in the framework of the distant past. Daniel or Noah or Enoch is made to predict situations and developments that are contemporaneous with the author and with the times of the book's first readers. This enables the apocalyptist to speak to the present with all the authority of hoary antiquity.

John of Patmos does not locate his visions in the distant past. They apply to the immediate future. The "revelation of Jesus Christ" is to show God's servants "what must soon take place" (1:1). An angel bids the seer: "Do not seal up the words of the prophecy of this book, for the time is near" (22:10; cf. 1:3).

Finally, in contrast to Jewish apocalypses Revelation has the format of a letter. Chapters 1–3 consist of a covering letter followed by letters to seven churches. The epistolary form is superimposed on the whole by delaying the benediction to the very end: "The grace of the Lord Jesus be with all the saints" (22:21). 1:3 makes clear that John expects the book to be read aloud in the various congregations—much as Paul at an earlier time intended his letters to be read to assembled groups of Christians.

Occasion, Date, Address

The occasion of Revelation was an attempt by the Roman imperial authorities to revive and enforce the cult of emperor worship. John pictures the Roman Empire as a seven-headed beast rising out of the sea (13:1). The imperial priesthood is represented as a second beast, having two horns like a lamb (simulating the Messiah) but with the voice of a dragon (betraying its Satanic origin). Working great wonders and imposing economic sanctions, it endeavors to enforce the universal observance of Caesar worship (13:11-17). The Christians at Smyrna are warned that persecution for their faith is at hand (2:10). Christians at Philadelphia are told that the hour of trial is about to come upon the whole world (3:10). Reference is made to many who have been slain for their faith (6:9). One martyr is cited by name (2:13).

In the early 60's Nero began a violent persecution of Christians at Rome. However, this was restricted to Rome and had nothing to do with the issue of emperor worship. The first emperor who seems to have tried to make Christians participate in Caesar worship was Domitian (81-96). The earliest reference to the date of Revelation is by Irenaeus around 180. He placed the composition of the book toward the end of Domitian's reign. Most scholars today agree that the internal evidence supports a date during the early 90's.

If we could solve the puzzles involved in the number of the beast in 13:18 and in the mysterious reckoning in 17:9-12 we might be more certain of the date of the book. Unfortunately we do not have the "mind with wisdom" that no doubt most of John's first readers possessed. It may be that 13:3 is an allusion to the widespread belief that Nero did not commit suicide in 68 and would later return to afflict the Rome he had ruled as a tyrant. Possibly this belief in a Nero come to life again was combined with the doctrine of the Antichrist in 13:8. Further, it may be that some belief in Domitian as the reincarnation of Nero underlies 17:11.

But all this, however attractive, remains hypothetical.

Revelation probably comes from the later years of the reign of Domitian—yet an earlier or later date cannot be ruled out.

Some scholars view 6:6 as a protest against, or at any rate a reference to, a change of agricultural policy by Domitian (see comment). If this interpretation is correct, Revelation might be dated around 93.

The address in 1:4, 11 is to the seven churches in the Roman province of Asia (western Asia Minor). This, plus the seven letters in chapters 2–3, indicate that the intended readers were the Christians of the Asian churches. From extrabiblical sources it appears that the cult of emperor worship was enforced with particular zeal in the province of Asia. A new temple for the worship of Caesar was erected at Ephesus during Domitian's reign.

Authorship

The author refers to his own name on four occasions as John (1:1, 4, 9; 22:8). As early as the middle of the second century Justin Martyr identified the author with John the son of Zebedee. This identification was challenged late in the second century by Christian heretics and early in the third also by many orthodox leaders in western Christendom. Yet the view ultimately prevailed. In the fourth century this was more instrumental than anything else in determining the final acceptance of Revelation as a canonical book.

Early in the third century Dionysius, bishop of Alexandria, recognized that John the son of Zebedee, since he had written the gospel and the letters that bear his name, could not have written Revelation because its style, vocabulary, and ideas differ so greatly. This is a judgment in which most scholars today concur—though some hold that, if any of the New Testament writings can be ascribed to the apostle John, Revelation has a better claim than any other.

John himself tells us that at the time of his first vision he "was on the island called Patmos on account of the word of God and the testimony of Jesus" (1:9). Patmos was off the coast of Asia Minor west of the city of Miletus. The meaning may be simply that the author was engaged in missionary work there. But since the island is known to have been the site of a Roman penal colony, the traditional view that he was imprisoned there for his activities as a Christian missionary is probably correct.

In 1:1 he speaks of himself as a "servant" of God, or of Jesus Christ. In 1:9 he describes himself as a brother and companion of Asian Christians in their tribulation. In his letters to the seven churches and throughout the book he writes with a sense of commission and authority. This implies that he himself belonged to the province of Asia, that he was well known to the readers of his book, and that he exercised some measure of jurisdiction over Asian churches. His imperfect command of Greek and the many Semitisms that occur in his writing support the assumption that he was a Jewish Christian who still thought in Aramaic. With these facts about the John of Revelation we must be content.

The Message

John's revelation is primarily an appeal for resistance to all demands of the cult of emperor worship. The glories and privileges of martyrdom are extolled throughout the book. The souls of those who have been slain are sheltered beneath the heavenly altar. Their prayers for vengeance on the non-Christian world have been heard. Martyrs have already been granted their spiritual bodies and are assured that soon their predestined number will be filled (6:9-11). A voice from heaven declares that all who will die as Christians are blessed (14:13). The author sees them standing by the glassy sea in heaven, singing a song of praise to God as did Moses and his followers (15:2-4). They participate with the Lamb in the last war against paganism (19:14). They reign with him for a thousand years as judges, priests, and kings, and they escape the second death (20:6).

The author is certain that the Roman Empire and the cult of emperor worship are shortly to be destroyed. The demonic plagues that are to come upon the empire are portrayed in lurid colors. Rome is symbolized as a great harlot seated on many

waters and drunk with the blood of the saints and martyrs of
Jesus (17:1-6). John beholds the city wasted in civil strife (17:16).
An angel foretells its doom (18:1-3). Christians are urged to
leave the city lest they share the impending disaster (18:4). The
"saints and apostles and prophets" in heaven are exhorted to
gloat over the judgment God has wrought (18:20). Merchants,
shipowners, and mariners, whose prosperity depends on their
Roman trade, will view the disaster with amazement and
despair (18:11-19).

An angelic host in heaven sings a hymn of praise that God has
been avenged. God has passed judgment on the city, which by
its imperial cult has corrupted the earth with idolatry (19:1-2).
An anticipated eighth emperor and his supporters will be
conquered by the Lamb and his followers (17:11, 14). In the end
the emperor and his false prophet—the representative of the
cult of Caesar worship—will be cast alive into the fiery lake of
brimstone. Their allies, the kings of the earth and their armies,
will be slain by the sword of the lamb (19:19-21).

The Church

Christians form a community of redeemed people, purchased
for God from every linguistic, racial, and national group by the
sacrificial death of Christ. The seal of God on their foreheads will
protect them from the demonic plagues which will afflict the
pagan world (7:3). Under the symbolism of 144,000 drawn in
equal numbers from the ideal twelve tribes they are pictured as
the true Israel of God which is to be saved from the coming woes
(7:1-8).

In a succeeding vision the same community appears as an
innumerable multitude from all nations. They will constitute
the ultimate society of those who have been redeemed from the
"great tribulation." In a vision John beholds them praising and
serving God day and night in the temple, guided and comforted
by Christ (7:9-17). They are "those who are invited to the
marriage supper of the Lamb" (19:9). In the new Jerusalem they
will see God's face, bear the divine name on their foreheads, and
worship God as servants (22:3-4).

The true church for John is made up of all who have refused or will refuse to worship the statue of the emperor. Those who suffer captivity or martyrdom are predestined to do so (13:10). In fact all who will inherit the new Jerusalem have had their names "written in the Lamb's book of life" (21:27). Martyrs are a preferred group within the true church. John believes that all Christians in the coming evil period of conflict will suffer martyrdom (13:15). The faithful of earlier days who have died a natural death will join them in the new heaven and the new earth after the resurrection and the judgment that are to follow the millenial age (20:11-15).

Some General Observations

Revelation is drama of a high order set on a cosmic stage. Despite its author's faulty Greek his book rises again and again to heights of sublimity and grandeur. It has inspired some of the world's greatest literature, poetry, and art. Though he has drawn heavily on Old Testament symbolism and imagery and occasionally on pagan mythology (cf. chapter 12), he has made this borrowed material his own. He has created a work of singular vividness, power, and intensity.

The God of Revelation is represented as a heavenly oriental king. God's righteous judgments will fall on enemies and on those who oppress the faithful. But God is not just a God of wrath and retribution. God is also a God who can enter into tender relations with people. God will wipe away every tear from their eyes in the day that sorrow and death will be no more. God will make them kings and priests, and they will serve God every day in the temple.

The Christ of Revelation shares the throne with God. He is a divine being, and titles ascribed to him are often not to be distinguished from those applied to God. He holds the "keys of Death and Hades" (1:18). He is "Lord of lords and King of kings" (17:14). He is "the Alpha and the Omega, the first and the last, the beginning and the end" (22:13). His most characteristic title is the "Lamb," or "Lamb of God." This refers in part to the significance of his death. He was the sacrificial victim by whose blood the faithful are redeemed. In part it refers to his role as vicegerent, or agent, of God. In this latter sense "Lamb of God" is interchangeable with "Lion of Judah."

We are reminded incidentally that Jesus Christ was descended from David (22:16), that he was of the Jewish race (5:5), that he was crucified (11:8), and that he rose from the dead. That is virtually all that is left of the gospel portrait. In its place is that of a divine warrior who will overcome all his enemies. Seated on a white horse, clad in a robe dipped in blood, and followed by heavenly armies, he will triumph at last in the hard-fought battle (19:11-16).

John represents Christianity as a moral religion. He condemns idolatry, theft, uncleanness, and falsehood. He stresses the virtues of chastity, loyalty, patience, endurance, faith, and zeal. But the reader will note that there is scarcely an echo of the Sermon on the Mount in the book. Nothing is said of love for one's enemies. On the contrary there is bitter hatred. The situation for which the book was written in part accounts for this bitterness.

As an apocalypse Revelation is concerned with the events of its own time and with those that its author expected to take place in the immediate future. To understand its message we must keep its literary and theological affiliation in mind. We must also relate it to the historical and religious situation in the Roman Empire—especially in the province of Asia toward the close of the first century.

Apocalypses were not written for a people or a church hundreds or thousands of years later than their time of writing. They were written for their own day and generation. Like other apocalyptic seers, John believed that history had about run its course. It was about to be interrupted by the dramatic and catastrophic introduction of the kingdom of God. Therefore the message of Revelation for the reader today is indirect rather than direct. Perhaps it may be expressed in the words of James Russell Lowell:

Though the cause of Evil prosper, yet 'tis Truth alone is strong.

Truth forever on the scaffold, Wrong forever on the throne,—
Yet that scaffold sways the future, and, behind the dim unknown,
Standeth God within the shadow, keeping watch above his own.

I. PROLOGUE (1:1-3)

Probably the original title of the work was this entire
prologue, or possibly its opening words: **The Revelation of
Jesus Christ.** "The Revelation of John" and **The Revelation to
John** are variant translations of a second century superscription.
In the prologue the author wishes to stress that the revelation to
follow was given by **God** to **Jesus Christ**. It was mediated by the
latter to the author through the agency of an **angel**. He expects
the **words of the prophecy** to be read **aloud** in congregational
assemblies. Then he pronounces a blessing on the reader and on
the listeners, provided they pay attention to **what is written
therein.**

II. EXHORTATION TO THE ASIAN CHURCHES (1:4–3:22)

A. A COVERING LETTER (1:4-20)

A covering letter is prefixed to the following seven letters in
chapters 2–3. These were addressed to churches in the Roman
province of Asia (see Introduction)—possibly congregations
under the author's special oversight.

1:4-8. *Salutation and Ascription.* At the very beginning we
are introduced to the sacred number **seven**. It is the symbol of
wholeness or perfection which determines so much of the
structure of the book. As in Paul's letters, **grace** is substituted
for the secular "greetings." **Peace** carries overtones of the
Semitic word for "salvation." The greetings come from three
sources. **He who is and who was and who is to come** is probably
an expansion of God's name as given in Exodus 3:14: "I AM WHO
I AM." The reference to the **seven spirits who are before his**

throne may have been influenced by the idea of seven archangels in late Jewish angelology. But the number corresponds also to the seven spirits of Persian Zoroastrianism. The word for **witness** can also mean "martyr." In its present reference to **Jesus Christ** it should probably be so translated.

1:5b-8. Verses 5b-6 refer of course to Christ. Verse 7 draws on the imagery of Daniel 7:13 but reinterprets the passage to apply to Christ and his imminent second coming (see below on verses 12-13a). God is represented as the speaker in verse 8 (cf. 21:6). **Alpha** and **Omega** are the names of the first and last letters in the Greek alphabet. The clause is synonymous with "the first and the last, the beginning and the end," which appears in 22:13 referring to Jesus.

1:9-20. *The Commission to Write.* John presents his credentials as a prophet and seer. He does not claim to be an apostle, a bishop, or an elder. He is only a **brother** who shares in the persecution, the fortitude, and the triumph of his fellow Christians. On **Patmos** see Introduction. Assuming the usual interpretation that John is a prisoner, his statement that he is on the island **on account of the word of God and the testimony of Jesus** means that he has been banished because of his loyalty to the Christian cause. He has refused to deny Christ and worship the emperor.

1:10-11. John claims that his vision took place when he was in a mystical trance **on the Lord's day**. Here is the first reference in literature to the first day of the week as the Christian holy day. As in Paul's description of the appearance of Christ in the last days (I Thessalonians 4:16), John's heavenly Lord speaks to him with a **loud voice** that sounds like **trumpet** blast. **Book** should probably be translated "scroll" here as it is in chapters 5 and 10.

1:12-13a. John's loose Greek in verse 12a justifies the New English Bible translation "I turned to see whose voice it was that spoke to me." The **seven golden lampstands** are identified in verse 20 as symbolic of the seven churches. The phrase **one like a son of man** is used in Daniel 7:13. There it means the faithful remnant of the Jewish people—or possibly some representative of the nation, conceivably its patron angel Michael. In various intertestamental writings, however, "son of man" designates God's heavenly vicegerent in the last days. This latter meaning is found in the Synoptic gospels and determines its usage in John's revelation.

1:13b-16. The portrayal of the heavenly Christ as one **clothed with a long robe and with a golden girdle round his breast** was suggested by the description of the angel in Daniel 10:5-6—as were also the references to **his eyes** as a **flame of fire** and **his feet . . . like burnished bronze**. That **his head and his hair** are **white as white wool** is drawn from the description of God as the "ancient of days" in Daniel 7:9. **Many waters** is appropriately translated "rushing waters" by the New English Bible. **In his right hand** the heavenly Christ **held seven stars**. These are identified in verse 20 as the angels of the seven churches. But they also symbolize Christ's power over the seven planets that in popular astrology determined the destinies of people.

The **sharp two-edged sword** proceeding **from his mouth** suggests both a warrior who smites the foe and a judge who annihilates them with the sentence of judgment. The simile of Christ's countenance as the **sun shining in full strength** is probaby drawn from Judges 5:31. Some interpreters hold that John's imagery is also intended to portray Christ in terms to surpass a current description of the sun god Mithra.

1:17-18. Prostration following the manifestation of the supernatural is a familiar feature of accounts of visions. It is usually followed by some word of reassurance. Here the author probably had in mind Daniel 10:9-11. **I am the first and the last** (cf. verse 8) is derived from Isaiah 44:6 and 48:12, where the clause is used by God as a self-designation. Here it is expanded in light of the crucifixion and resurrection and is used by the heavenly Christ of himself—as also in 2:8 and, in part, in 22:13.

Hades for this author is not the Greek place of punishment but the Hebrew Sheol, thought of as a subterranean pit where the souls of both good and evil dwell after death. **Death** is the state and **Hades** is the place of the dead. Both are personified in 6:8 and 20:13. Since they have been overcome by Christ, he can be pictured as holding the **keys** with which, at the time of the end, he can release his faithful followers.

1:19-20. Verse 19 resumes and amplifies the command given in verse 11. The **seven lampstands** (cf. verse 12) are identified with the **seven churches** that are to be addressed. The **seven stars** are said to represent their guardian **angels.** As nations have their special angelic patrons (cf. Daniel 10:13, 20-21), so have the seven congregations of the province of Asia. The covering letter appears to end without the benediction customary in other New Testament writings that are in letter form. But John may think of the letter as applying to the whole book and as concluding with the grace in 22:21.

B. LETTERS TO SEVEN CHURCHES (2:1–3:22)

2:1-7. *Ephesus.* In the first century Ephesus was the fourth largest city in the Roman Empire and capital of the province of Asia. Located on the Aegean coast at the mouth of a small river, it served as the western terminus of a long caravan route from the far east by way of Palestine and Syria. It was "temple keeper of the great Artemis" (Acts 19:35), the goddess whose Ephesian shrine was one of the wonders of the world. It was also a major center for the promotion of emperor worship. In the early 50's Paul had founded the church in the city and had ministered there longer than anywhere else. The fact that the Ephesian congregation is named first among the seven indicates its importance in John's day.

2:1b-5. The letter contains a mixture of praise and criticism. The church is commended for its vigorous action against **false teachers** and its fortitude under suffering. It is also blamed for having lost the earlier warmth of its **love**—probably referring to communal love rather than to devotion to Christ.

2:6-7. Censure is lessened by acknowledging the hatred of the Ephesian Christians for the practices of the **Nicolaitans.** These were probably the false **apostles,** or itinerant missionaries, of verse 2, whose special vices are condemned in verses 14-15. The

Nicolaitans were believed to have been followers of Nicolaus, the proselyte of Antioch who was early made a deacon of the church (Acts 6:5). Verse 7a is a formula in all the letters and relates each to the readers of the whole book. The **tree of life** is the symbol of immortality. According to 22:2 it stands in the street of the heavenly Jerusalem, for which the **paradise of God** is therefore a synonym.

2:8-11. *Smyrna.* The city of Smyrna was north of Ephesus. It lay at the head of a deep gulf of the Aegean and at the end of a road leading across Lydia from Phrygia and the East. Long an ally of Rome, it dedicated a temple to the goddess Roma as early as 195 B.C. and in A.D. 23 was granted the right to erect a temple to the Emperor Tiberius. It is not known when or by whom the church at Smyrna was founded. A mid-second century writing tells of the martyrdom at Smyrna of Polycarp, an aged bishop of the church.

2:8b-9. This second letter has nothing but praise for the congregation at Smyrna. Though they are persecuted and poverty-stricken from the confiscation of their property, these Christians can still be described as **rich** in spiritual possessions. The reference to false **Jews** (cf. 3:9) is usually understood as a bitter comment based on the church's claim to be the true Israel. But there is another possibility. Jews were exempted by Rome from participating in emperor worship. This may be John's condemnation of Christians who seek to escape persecution by claiming to be Jews.

2:10-11. The seer predicts that the church is about to suffer a brief but still more violent affliction. He anticipates that it may lead to martyrdom for many. The ultimate power behind the persecuting Roman state is the **devil**. The Christian's reward for martyrdom is a **crown of life**, a metaphor borrowed from the wreath awarded to a victor in competitive games and symbolizing immortality. Martyrs are to be spared the **second death**. This is explained in 20:14-15 and 21:8 as the eternal death of those condemned at the last judgment.

2:12-17. *Pergamum.* Pergamum is located northeast of Smyrna. It had long been the capital of the province of Asia when Augustus moved the seat of government to Ephesus. It was noted as a religious center, with shrines to Zeus, Athena, Dionysus, and Asclepius, the Greek god of healing. More especially it was also the major center in Asia of the cult of emperor worship. In 29 B.C. it dedicated a temple to the "divine Augustus and the goddess Roma." This symbolized for Christians the threat to the existence of the church and no doubt explains the reference to **Satan's throne**.

2:12b-13. The congregation is praised for its loyalty, especially for its steadfastness when a certain **Antipas** was put to death. Throughout his apocalypse John anticipates that many believers will suffer martyrdom. Antipas is the only one he cites as having already died for his faith.

2:14-17. A warning is added to the praise. There are those in the church **who hold the teaching of Balaam**. On the basis of Numbers 31:16 Balaam had long been regarded as the prototype of corrupt teachers. Here the Balaamites are closely linked with the **Nicolaitans** (see above on 2:6-7). Both may be understood as meaning "destroyers of the people." They are accused of sexual immorality and of eating meat sold on the market after the animal was sacrificed to pagan gods. If they persist in their practices, they are threatened with destruction at Christ's imminent return.

On the other hand, those who remain faithful will be fed in the new age with **manna**, as the Israelites were after their deliverance from Egypt (cf. Exodus 16). They will be given an amulet, or charm, to protect them against every evil. The **new name** is probably that of Christ or God. Some interpret it as a secret name given to the faithful person.

2:18-29. *Thyatira*. Located about forty miles southeast of Pergamum, Thyatira was unimportant as a political and religious center. Yet it was a prosperous industrial town, noted among other things for the manufacture and dyeing of woolen goods (cf. Acts 16:14). In his opening description of the **Son of God** (cf. 1:13b-16) John may be contrasting him with the sun god Apollo, the special diety worshiped at Thyatira.

2:19-23. John commends the congregation for its **patient**

endurance under persecution. But he blames it for tolerating a false **prophetess**, to whom he gives the symbolic name **Jezebel**, after Ahab's immoral and idolatrous queen (cf. I Kings 16:31; 18:13; 19:1-2; 21:1-16). Her teachings and example are similar to those of the Nicolaitans (see above on 2:14-15). John forecasts her punishment as a warning to **all the churches**. The reference to **her children** is probably to her followers rather than to any adulterous offspring.

2:24-29. Those unaffected by this woman's vicious belief and behavior are urged to **hold fast.** It is uncertain to what **deep things of Satan** refers. Early heretics known as Gnostics claimed to have access to depths of knowledge denied the uninitiated, and some interpreters believe that John has replaced "of God" with "of Satan." Others believe that those concerned claimed they could probe the depths of evil without thereby contaminating themselves. Still others relate the phrase to John's overriding horror of emperor worship, whose devotees could be described as having plumbed Satanic depths. The faithful are promised a share in Christ's final victory. To what the gift of the **morning star** refers is not certain. At any rate it is intended to symbolize the immortal life that the faithful will receive from Christ.

3:1-6. *Sardis.* Some thirty miles southeast of Thyatira, Sardis was the former capital of the ancient kingdom of Lydia. It reached the peak of its prosperity during the reign of the fabulous Croesus about 560 B.C. Under Persian rule it fell into decline, but recovered some of its earlier importance under the Romans. The city was devastated by an earthquake in A.D. 17 and rebuilt through the generosity of Tiberius. It competed for the honor of erecting a temple to the emperor, but lost out to Smyrna. Early Greek historians accused the citizens of Sardis of luxury and immorality.

3:1b-3. In John's day the church has fallen into a state of apathy, and he charges it with being spiritually **dead.** In words that recall those of Jesus in the gospels (see Mark 13:33) he summons the Christians at Sardis to recall what they have **received and heard**, to hold that fast, and to **repent.** If they are not on the watch, Christ's second coming will overtake them as a **thief** in the night (cf. Matthew 24:43-44; I Thessalonians 5:2-4).

3:4-5. Yet, with all the church's lethargy, there are still a **few** at Sardis who have kept themselves free of immorality. These are promised a fitting reward; they are to be Christ's companions in the messianic kingdom. They will be robed **in white garments** as a symbol of their purity—an idea conventional in ancient thought. Some interpreters believe that the author had in mind some such notion of the resurrection body as that to which Paul refers in II Corinthians 5:4. The names of the victors will be preserved in the **book of life**. The belief that God keeps a heavenly register has been traced by some to the influence on Jewish thought of astrological speculation. However, the concept is a familiar one in the Old Testament, in intertestamental literature, elsewhere in the New Testament, and often in this book (13:8; 17:8; 20:12, 15; 21:27).

3:6. The heavenly Christ assures those who are victorious in a life of Christian loyalty that they will be acknowledged before God and the angelic hosts in the day of judgment. These words are reminiscent of Matthew 10:32 and Luke 12:8.

3:7-13. *Philadelphia.* A city about thirty miles to the southeast of Sardis, Philadelphia was of commercial rather than political importance. It suffered like Sardis from the earthquake of A.D. 17 and was also given a generous donation from imperial funds to assist in rebuilding.

3:7b-9. The letter, like that to Smyrna, is one of praise and encouragement. There is no censure. The **key of David** points back to 1:18. Together with what follows it is also a quotation from Isaiah 22:22. As Eliakim during the reign of Hezekiah had authority to open and shut the house of David, so the heavenly Christ can open and shut the door of God's kingdom. The **open door** may refer to opportunity for missionary work. More probably it is an assurance of entrance into the new age. On verse 9 see above on 2:8b-9.

3:10-13. Despite their numerical weakness the Philadelphians have shown fortitude under persecution. They will be brought safely through the **hour of trial** that is shortly to beset all non-Christians. The person who remains faithful will be made a **pillar** in God's temple. Since the language is metaphorical, there need be no inconsistency between this statement and the declaration in 21:22 that God and the Lamb are to be the only temple in the heavenly Jerusalem. Christ will imprint a **name** on the victor (cf. 2:17; 14:1; 22:4)—that of God and Christ and that of the **New Jerusalem**, the messianic city that is to descend after the last judgment and the creation of the new heaven and the new earth (cf. 21:1-2). According to 19:12, 16 Christ's **new name** will not be revealed until his second coming. It will be "King of kings and Lord of lords."

3:14-22. *Laodicea.* Laodicea was situated about fifty miles southeast of Philadelphia in the valley of a tributary of the Meander River called the Lycus. It was an important commercial, banking, and medical center. The congregation at Laodicea had been founded as early as Paul's day (cf. Colossians 2:1; 4:13-16) and Paul intimates that he wrote it a letter (Colossians 4:16). This has either been lost or, as some believe, is the little letter known as Philemon.

3:14*b*-18. It is the apathy of the entire congregation which troubles the seer, and to which he directs the censure of the heavenly Christ. Christ is given the title **the Amen**, and is called the **beginning of God's creation**. This phrase probably recalls the "first-born of the dead" in 1:5 rather than some doctrine of his preexistence as in Colossians 1:15. The loyalty of Laodicean Christians is scathingly characterized as **lukewarm**. Their complacency in their material well-being is ridiculed, and they are counseled to purchase true spiritual riches. Many interpreters see in verses 17-18 references to Laodicean wealth based on banking and the manufacture of woolen goods—and to a popular eye medicine known as "Phrygian powder" that was used in the Laodicean medical school.

3:19-22. The tone of the letter now changes abruptly from censure to appeal. The bitter words were utterances of reproving and chastening **love**. But the summons to repentance is urgent. Christ's second coming is at hand. In language that recalls such passages as Mark 13:29 and Luke 12:36 the heavenly Lord declares: **I stand at the door and knock.**

The idea that God's new age would be inaugurated with a banquet at which the redeemed would feast together with the Messiah is a familiar one in Jewish intertestamental literature. It is also reflected in Jesus' words in Luke 12:35-38 and Mark 14:25. The thought of the heavenly Christ on a **throne** occurs also in other New Testament writings. The seer depicts the fulfillment of Christ's promise to the faithful that they will **sit with me on my throne** when he speaks in 20:4 of the martyrs reigning with Christ for a thousand years.

III. The Revelation of Things to Come (4:1–22:5)

The letters of chapters 1–3 have sought to fortify and encourage Christians who have experienced or are about to experience persecution for their Christian faith. There have been threats to apostates of fearful punishment. There have been promises to the faithful of glorious immortality with Christ in God's kingdom—especially to those who will suffer martyrdom for their loyalty. The second major division of the book now depicts how these threats and promises are to be fulfilled. The benediction in 22:21 was evidently intended to give an epistolary format to the whole work. Only chapters 4–22 are apocalyptic—"revelation of things to come"—in the strict sense of the word. However, the material in chapter 1 gives such a setting to the letters also.

A. Prelude in Heaven (4:1–5:14)

Chapters 4–5 consist of visions of God enthroned in heaven, surrounded by worshiping hosts and angelic attendants. God gives the divine book to Christ, the Lamb. The scenes assure Christian readers that God and Christ are shortly to intervene in the affairs of this age. They will deliver the faithful from the domination of Satan and demonic powers—both superhuman demons and the demonic forces embodied in the Roman state and the priesthood of the imperial cult.

4:1-11. *Vision of God on The Throne.* The formula **After this I looked, and lo** is the seer's way of introducing a new vision (cf. 7:1, 9; 15:5; 18:1). In terms of the cosmology of antiquity John thinks of a solid vault arching over the flat earth, with heaven located above the vault and Hades a pit below the earth. While the notion of seven heavens occurs in much Jewish intertestamental writing, in this book there is only a single heaven. The seer, who has heretofore been on earth, is admitted to **heaven** by an **open door** in the sky. The **first voice** that bids him **come up** is presumably Christ's as in 1:10. The feat of levitation is accomplished in a state of spiritual ecstasy or trance.

As often in Jewish and Christian literature, and as customarily in this book, God is represented as **seated on the throne.** No attempt is made at direct description. John views only the splendor of light encircling the throne, which he compares to that of precious stones passing through a cloud and emerging as a **rainbow** of **emerald** green.

4:4. The **twenty-four elders** on their **thrones** are God's heavenly court. Some interpreters believe they represent angelic kings, though such a hierarchy in this precise form and number is not mentioned in Jewish literature. Others trace their origin in the seer's thought to astrological speculation of twenty-four stars outside the circle of the zodiac, stars that functioned as judges of the world. Another guess is that they are the heavenly counterpart of the twenty-four groups of priests and the twenty-four details of Levites who ministered in turn in the temple in Jerusalem. Still others think that John's reference to **thrones** and **white garments** and **crowns** means that he has Christian martyrs in mind.

4:5-6a. The description of God's manifestation is resumed. This imagery is often used in the book to suggest God's awful power and majesty (8:5; 11:19; 16:18). The **seven torches of fire** are probably suggested to begin with by the seven planetary gods of popular astrology. Here they are identified as the **seven**

spirits of God, mentioned in 1:4. In 3:1 these spirits are said to belong to Christ.

4:6*b***-8***a***.** The **four living creatures** are described for the most part as being like the cherubim of Ezekiel 1. But John's description has also been influenced by Isaiah's vision of the seraphim in Isaiah 6. They represent the highest order of angels for this New Testament writing. The concept of the cherubim as four-winged guardian powers with faces of a **lion**, an **ox**, a **man**, and an **eagle** comes from Babylonian sources and is ultimately dependent on the four signs of the zodiac. Isaiah's seraphim with **six wings** were angelic representations of lightning or fire.

The reference to **eyes all round and within** is borrowed from Ezekiel, who had in mind, not the creatures themselves, but wheels that accompanied them in flight. Here "within" probably means on the under side of the wings. The many eyes symbolize the all-seeing intelligence of the creatures.

4:8*b***-***d***.** The song of these creatures comes from the hymn of the seraphim in Isaiah 6:3. John's modifications introduce attributes of God that he stresses throughout his book: **the Lord God Almighty**. It may be that the seer delighted in this name because it overshadowed the title "Our Lord and God" which had been assumed by the Emperor Domitian. John would regard this as blasphemy. In any case the name asserts John's conviction of the ultimate triumph of righteousness. The latter half of the song reproduces the title already given to God in 1:4.

4:9-11. In verse 8 the praise of the living creatures has been said to be continuous. Now it is represented as breaking forth at intervals (cf. 5:8, 14; 11:16; 19:4). But this is a minor inconsistency in an imposing and magnificent scene. **Glory and honor and thanks** summarize the praise of the living creatures. At this the twenty-four elders prostrate themselves and make their response. When they **cast their crowns before the throne**, they acknowledge that all their kingly dignity is derived from and subordinate to God. It is very likely that their hymn to the glory of God as creator belonged already in John's time to the liturgy of the church.

5:1-5. *Vision of the Sealed Scroll.* The seer's attention is now directed to a sealed **scroll** (see above on 1:10-11) that lies in God's **right hand.** Since in a rolled scroll only a portion of the outside writing is visible, the conclusion that it holds writing also on the inside, however obvious, can be only an assumption. It is not clear how John thinks of the scroll as **sealed with seven seals**—the perfect number again. Either the entire roll cannot be opened until all seven seals are broken or, more probably, in some way each of the scroll's seven sections is separately sealed. As in Daniel 8:26, the book of destiny has been sealed to keep its contents secret until the time of revelation should come. John may have drawn his imagery in part from such passages as Isaiah 29:11 and Daniel 8:26. But it is dependent largely on Ezekiel 2:9-10.

5:2-5. The scroll contains God's judgments that John is to reveal in the following visions. The **angel** is described as **strong** because his appeal for someone **worthy to open the scroll** is uttered in a **voice** that can penetrate to the farthest limits of **heaven** and **earth** and **under the earth**, or Hades. The seer reports that he **wept** because there appears to be no one in the whole of God's creation whose rank and office give them the right to open the scroll. Thus the promise of a revelation to him of what is to take place (4:1) will remain unredeemed. But **one of the elders** assuages his grief. There is one uniquely qualified by his office to **open the scroll** and to break **its seven seals**—the Messiah, the Christ.

The victor is described as the **Lion of the tribe of Judah.** This comes from a messianic interpretation of Genesis 49:9, "Judah is a lion's whelp." The **Root of David** is taken from the messianic meaning of Isaiah 11:1: "There shall come forth a shoot from the stump of Jesse, and a branch shall grow out of his roots." Christ's descent from David may be presupposed in 3:7, but is explicitly mentioned elsewhere in this book only in 22:16. In each instance it belongs to the liturgical inheritance of the church rather than to John's own particular doctrine.

5:6-14. *Vision of the Lamb.* In this passage the **Lamb** is introduced as another name for the risen Christ. It occurs a total of twenty-nine times in the book and is therefore John's characteristic title for the heavenly Lord. In this respect Revelation and the Gospel of John have a christological element in common, though the presentations of the figure of the Lamb differ in detail.

Nowhere in Revelation is the title used to allude to Christ's meekness or gentleness. In this chapter the Lamb is the object of the worship offered by the hosts of heaven and earth. In chapter 6 he opens the book of destiny. In 7:9-11 he is enthroned with God and receives the praise of a countless host. In 13:8 and 21:27 he has charge of the book of life. In 14:1 he stands on Mt. Zion with the 144,000 of the redeemed. In 17:14 he is the victor over the armies of the Antichrist. In 19:7 the multitude of the redeemed celebrate his marriage to the glorified church. In 21:22-23 the Lord God and the Lamb are the temple of the new Jerusalem and the Lamb is the lamp by which God's glory illuminates the city. In 22:1 the water of the river of life in the new age issues from the throne of God and of the Lamb.

But the term designates not only the conquering and triumphant Christ but also one "with the marks of slaughter upon him" (New English Bible; cf. 13:8). The portrayal of the Messiah as a lamb is found occasionally in Jewish intertestamental literature. But the inclusion here and in the Gospel of John of the idea of a redeeming sacrifice is due no doubt to a messianic interpretation of Isaiah 53:6-7: "All we like sheep have gone astray; . . . and the LORD has laid on him the iniquity of us all. . . . Like a lamb that is led to the slaughter, . . . so he opened not his mouth."

5:6. The position of the Lamb is in immediate proximity to the **throne**, "inside the circle of living creatures and the circle of the elders" (New English Bible). It is useless to try to harmonize the various metaphors John uses for the celestial Lord: the Lion of Judah, the Root of David, and the **Lamb . . . with seven horns and with seven eyes**. The terms are symbolic rather than representative. The Lion of Judah and the Root of David designate Christ as the expected Davidic Messiah (see above on 5:2-5). Since the horn is a common Old Testament symbol of power, Christ's **seven horns** suggest power that is full and complete. His **seven eyes**, identified with the **seven spirits of God sent out into all the earth**, symbolize his omniscience. All this is combined with the thought of Christ's self-sacrifice on the cross as the avenue to that full power and knowledge.

5:7-8. By virtue of his office the Lamb takes the scroll of destiny (cf. verses 1-5). The heavenly court of angels and representatives of God's people respond with homage and adoration. The **harp**, literally "lyre," is the instrument of praise. The **golden bowls full of incense** are equated with the **prayers of the saints**—the supplications of God's people on earth for the speedy consummation of the divine will.

5:9-10. The **new song** possibly depends on Isaiah 42:10. The heavenly court praises the Lamb as **worthy** to open the scroll and avenge God's people—worthy because his death has purchased **men for God from every tribe and tongue and people and nation**. This last is a description of the multiracial church of John's day. As in 1:6, the promise is that faithful Christians will reign in God's **kingdom** and serve God as **priests**—a promise whose fulfillment in the millennium is further predicted in 20:6.

5:11-14. The adoration of the Lamb by the four living creatures and the twenty-four elders in verses 8-10 is followed by that of countless hosts of angels in verses 11-12 and by all God's creation in verse 13. The chapter ends with the response of **Amen** by the creatures and with an act of homage and worship by the elders.

B. The Seven Seals (6:1–8:1)

In this section the Lamb breaks the seals of the book of destiny one by one. The events recorded in the document are dramatically enacted. Nothing is said of reading the book. Its contents are made known by visual fulfillment. Some interpreters have looked for clues to the various woes in historical events that may have taken place during John's lifetime. Others have tried to understand them as an adaptation of ancient themes of oriental mythology. Still others have found references in some of the seven to great empires of the past.

Most scholars agree that John's imagery is based on the apocalyptic tradition reflected in Mark 13, Matthew 24, and Luke 21—war, famine, pestilence, persecution, and evidences of cosmic collapse. Whether he knew the gospels themselves may be questioned. The tradition behind these passages belonged to the common property of apocalyptic thought.

The underlying idea was that the coming of the end would be foretold by evidence that evil was rampant—evil in international affairs, in social life, and in the very structure of the universe. God would not intervene until the worst had come. Many authors took manifest pleasure in detailing the disasters to come. Though John has made use of the more or less stereotyped predictions of his predecessors, he has given them his own special arrangement and highly individual treatment. All this does not rule out the possibility that memories or experiences of historical events play some part in his predictions.

6:1-2. *A White Horse and Its Rider.* The opening of the first seal is accompanied by a thunderous command of the first of the four living creatures of the heavenly court: **"Come!"** Then a white horse appears, on which a crowned rider sits holding a bow. The imagery of this and of the three succeeding woes has evidently been suggested by the colored horses of Zechariah 1:8; 6:1-8. But John tranforms the functions of the Old Testament figures. Zechariah had represented them as God's messengers to the four quarters of the heaven with a mission to patrol the earth. Now they become God's agents of destruction.

The imagery of verse 2, its armed horseman presented with a **crown**, is clearly a personification of conquest. Interpreters differ on whether it is conquest in general or conquest of the Roman Empire by hordes of Parthian horsemen—of which many at that time stood in dread. The **bow** is known to have been the special weapon of the Parthians. However, the frequent mention in the Old Testament of the bow as the emblem of the warrior may be all that John has in mind.

6:3-4. *A Red Horse and Its Rider.* With the opening of the second seal a second living creature issues the order and a second rider appears on a red horse. He is given a **sword** and **permitted to take peace from the earth.** The color of the horse, the sword, and the mission clearly symbolize war. If the first episode symbolizes a war of conquest, the words **so that men should slay one another** suggest civil strife. Those who see an allusion to the Parthians in verses 1-2 sometimes see an allusion in these verses to the Romans. But the crown, bow, and sword are stereotyped symbols. The first rider is given a crown to symbolize conquest and the second a sword to foment civil strife.

6:5-6. *A Black Horse and Its Rider.* A third rider appears, mounted on a black horse and holding a **balance**—that is, a pair of scales. A voice announces: **A quart of wheat for a denarius . . .** The measure translated **quart** held enough grain to feed one person for a day. Though a **denarius** had a silver content of only about 20 cents, it represented a day's wage (cf. Matthew 20:2). With grain selling at such a price, the scene symbolizes the apocalyptic woe of famine. In the interests of Italian winegrowers Domitian issued an edict in 92 restricting the cultivation of vineyards in the provinces. He was compelled to revoke it because of opposition in Asia Minor. Some scholars see a reflection of this event in the final clause of verse 6.

6:7-8. *A Pale Horse and Its Rider.* The opening of the fourth seal is introduced by the now familiar formula. **Pale** represents a word translated "green" in 8:7, but the Moffatt translation "livid" suits the context better. **Death** and **Hades** (the Hebrew Sheol; see above on 1:17-18) are personified (cf. 20:13-14). Apparently they ride on the same beast. It has been suggested that originally John described a single rider, death in the sense of pestilence—the usual sequel to war, internal strife, and famine—who was **given power over a fourth of the earth.** It is thought that an editor influenced by 1:18 and 20:13-14 added Hades and the summary concluding verse 8.

6:9-11. *Lament of the Martyrs.* The opening of the fifth seal is followed by a vision of a different sort. The seer views the **souls**

of the faithful Christians who have already suffered martyrdom. They are in safekeeping beneath the **altar** in the heavenly temple, where they cry aloud for God's avenging judgment on the pagan world. They are told to wait in patience until the persecutions still to come fill up their required number. The idea that the end will not come until the predestined number of martyrs is **complete** is anticipated in earlier Jewish literature. In chapter 7 the seer declares that the number is 144,000.

6:12-17. *Shaking of the Universe.* The opening of the sixth seal is followed by a **great earthquake,** an eclipse of the sun, and other appalling portents of cosmic collapse. Terror-stricken people of every degree interpret them as signs that the last **day . . . has come.** The seer, however, thinks of them only as forerunners of the ultimate calamities. The language and imagery are familiar from Mark 13; Isaiah 34:4; Joel 2, and elsewhere. The statements in verse 14 that **every mountain and island was removed** and in verse 16 that the refugees call on the **mountains** to **fall on us** illustrate the author's use of hyperbole.

7:1-8. *Sealing of the Redeemed.* There is now a pause in the fearful succession of plagues. All that has gone before is preparatory to the breaking of the seventh seal—the event that will precipitate the awful final drama of the world's history. During this dramatic interlude the 144,000 of the spiritual Israel are **sealed** for their protection against demonic powers. John thinks of the earth as a vast square, with **four angels** at its **four corners** restraining the **four winds** that are to destroy it (cf. Isaiah 11:12; Ezekiel 7:2). No reference is made later in the book to these apocalyptic agencies. This is one of several indications that in this section the author is adapting material to his purpose from some source, clearly Jewish.

7:2-3. An **angel** rises out of the **East** bearing God's **seal**—God's signet ring. With this he imprints God's name or mark on the **foreheads** of those whose faithfulness is to be demonstrated by their martyrdom. Various prototypes may have influenced the author at this point. In Exodus 12 the firstborn of the Jews are protected against the destroyer by blood sprinkled on the doorposts of Jewish homes. In Isaiah 44:5

it is said that converts to Judaism will write God's name on their hands as evidence that they belong to him. The closest approximation is in Ezekiel 9:4, where one is to go "through Jerusalem, and put a mark upon the foreheads of the men who sigh and groan over all the abominations that are committed in it." Here the sealing of the redeemed on earth anticipates the reference to God's name on their foreheads in 22:4.

7:4-8. The **number of the sealed** is 144,000 (cf. 14:1), drawn in equal numbers from **every tribe of the sons of Israel.** If John is editing Jewish material, his source thought of the true Israel as a core of the Jewish faithful of all the ideal tribes. Here John interprets it to refer to Christians of every racial origin. Some believe verses 1-8 refer to Jewish Christians and verses 9-17 to their Gentile counterparts, but there is no ground for this. Both passages designate the same vast company. The square of twelve multiplied by a thousand is to be taken symbolically, no doubt representing the completeness and perfectness of God's people.

According to one count the Bible lists twenty different arrangements of the Jewish tribes, and this one agrees with none of them. The author puts **Judah** first in his list because elsewhere he traces Christ's descent through that patriarch (5:5). Curiously the tribe of Dan is omitted. Irenaeus, writing toward the end of the second century, asserted that the omission was due to the belief that the Antichrist would come from that tribe. John fills the gap left by the exclusion of Dan with **Manasseh,** the name of one of Joseph's sons.

7:9-17. *The Martyrs Before God's Throne.* The second vision in this interlude is not intended as a contrast to the first. The 144,000 symbolize the church as the true Israel on earth. The **great multitude which no man could number,** from all national, racial, and linguistic groups, is the church triumphant in heaven. It is the company of the glorified and victorious faithful awaiting the final consummation of God's purpose.

The vision is recounted by the seer to inspire the communities to which he is writing. The vast throng in heaven are those who will remain loyal despite the pressures of persecution and the threats of death. They stand in the presence of God and Christ, clothed as martyrs in **white robes** and carrying **palm branches** as symbols of thanksgiving and victory (cf. John 12:13). The theme of their praise is **salvation**—properly translated into our idiom in this context by the New English Bible as "victory." They joyously ascribe this victory to **God** and the **Lamb**, for neither they themselves nor any earthly powers could have overthrown the demonic hosts opposed to them.

7:11-12. The seer enumerates the concentric ranks of spiritual beings about the **throne**, from the outermost to the innermost. The innumerable host is presumably ranged around all these. The various heavenly orders prostrate themselves in homage to God. They make an antiphonal reply to the doxology of the church (verse 10) with their own sevenfold hymn of praise. The first **Amen!** is a response to the song of the church. The second is the liturgical conclusion to the doxology of the heavenly court.

7:13-14a. Serving as an "interpreting angel," **one of the elders** engages the seer in a dialogue. In the Old Testament this was often a formula for explaining a vision. **Sir**—"my lord"—represents the original meaning of the Greek term used of God and Christ. The seer cannot answer the elder's question until it is revealed that the heavenly company is identical with the 144,000.

7:14b. The visions in this chapter are in preparation for all that follows the breaking of the last seal. Therefore the reference to the **great tribulation** through which the company has passed must refer to all the woes that are still to be described rather than to one specific calamity. The statement that **they have washed their robes and made them white in the blood of the Lamb** asserts that deliverance and victory have been made possible because Christ, the first martyr, won that victory through his death.

7:15. The Greek verb translated **serve** means to perform the ritual service of the temple. The heavenly sanctuary will disappear at the final consummation. In the new heaven and the new earth God and the Lamb will be the only temple (21:22). But in the temple that now exists (chapters 4–5) all Christians are priests (1:6; 5:10). In turn God **will shelter them with his**

presence. The Hebrew word lying back of this last Greek phrase is *shekinah*. In Jewish literature *shekinah* meant the direct presence of God in the tabernacle or temple, in Jerusalem, or immediately overshadowing and protecting his people. Hence this text declares: "God will cause his *shekinah* to dwell upon the church in heaven."

7:16-17. The concluding verses of the scene are based in part on Isaiah 49:10. The thought of the Lamb as the shepherd of the church triumphant may well have been suggested by a memory of Psalm 23. The words with which the interpreter ends, the wonderful promise that **God will wipe away every tear from their eyes**, may have been prompted by Isaiah 25:8.

8:1. *A Half-Hour Silence in Heaven.* With the opening of the seventh seal there is an end to the praises and thanksgiving in heaven. The **silence** does not imply an interruption in the revelations given the seer. Possibly, as has been suggested, it is ordered so that the prayers of the suffering saints on earth, which concern God more than the praises of the angelic orders, may be laid before God (verses 3-5). Probably, however, the author's dramatic interest is enough to explain the introduction of the scene. The pause is an ominous prelude to the calamities that are to follow. No satisfactory explanation of the **half an hour** length of the heavenly silence has been given.

C. THE SEVEN TRUMPETS (8:2–11:19)

In a second group of seven the seer lists the seven catastrophes that follow the opening of the last seal. Seven plagues are released by blasts of the trumpets of doom.

8:2-6. *Fire Flung on the Earth.* **The seven angels who stand before God** may be the seven spirits mentioned in 1:4 and 4:5. More probably they are a new and distinct group who reflect the idea in late Jewish angelology of seven archangels. In I Enoch they are listed as Uriel, Raphael, Raguel, Michael, Sariel, Gabriel, and Remiel. In Jewish literature they are often called the "angels of the presence."

Raphael speaks of himself in Tobit 12:15 as "one of the seven holy angels who present the prayers of the saints and enter into the presence of the glory of the Holy one." In Luke 1:19 the angel who appears to Zechariah identifies himself as "Gabriel, who stand in the presence of God." Here the seven are God's ministering angels who carry out God's commands. The trumpet is the ram's horn, or *shophar,* an instrument to announce God's judgment. It is familiar in intertestamental literature and in such Old Testament passages as Isaiah 27:13.

8:3-6. Before the seven trumpets are blown there is the interlude of the **incense** offering. A nameless **angel** mixes the **prayers of all the saints** with **much incense** to offer them on the **altar** in the heavenly throne room. Like the prayers of the martyred souls under the altar (6:10), they are pleas for God's judgment. The scene is reminiscent of that portrayed in 5:8. Once the prayers have ascended with the smoke of the incense, the angel uses the **censer** in a new way. He hurls **fire from the altar . . . on the earth.** The act is followed by acts of nature (cf. 4:5) which imply that God has heard the prayers and will speedily give an answer. The sevenfold woe that issues from the seventh seal is about to break, and the seven angels prepare to sound their seven trumpets.

8:7. *A Shower of Bloody Hail and Fire.* Various Old Testament passages have suggested the author's images. In Joel 2:30 **blood** and **fire** are among the signs of the day of Yahweh. **Hail** mixed with fire is one of the plagues brought on Egypt preceding the exodus (Exodus 9:24). They serve as a model for the disasters which are now to precede God's deliverance of the people. After each of the first four and the sixth trumpet blasts a **third** of the objects affected are injured or destroyed.

8:8-9. *A Fiery Mountain Cast into the Sea.* In this second plague the turning of the sea into **blood** and the destruction of the fish are features taken from the first of the plagues in Egypt (Exodus 7:14-25). The ideas of a flaming mountain hurled into the sea and the wreck of a **third of the ships** are John's own contribution. On the basis of a passage in I Enoch some interpreters believe this mountain and the star in verse 10 represent wicked angels cast out of heaven to wreak destruction on the world.

8:10-11. *Pollution of the Waters.* The blast of the third trumpet is followed by the fall of a torchlike **star**—a meteor. It lands on a **third of the rivers** and the **fountains of water**. The scene is similar to the preceding one, and the idea of the corruption of the water is likewise taken from the first Egyptian plague. The name given to the blazing star is a puzzle. No star, meteor, or fallen angel is called **Wormwood** in any other ancient writing known. It may have been suggested by Jeremiah's use of this bitter plant as a symbol of divine punishment (Jeremiah 9:15; 23:15). That the **waters became wormwood** means that they were polluted with the juice of the plant. Wormwood is not a poison, but John was not concerned with such fine distinctions.

8:12. *A Partial Eclipse.* The blowing of the fourth trumpet results in a darkenig of a **third** of the **light** of the **sun** and the **moon** and the **stars**. The consequence is curious and illogical. There is a diminution not of the intensity but of the duration of the light. There is darkness for a **third of the day** and for a **third of the night**. The author is intent on describing the awesome effect of the scene as a whole, without concerning himself overly much with realistic detail. However startling he may have thought it, this plague does not match the others in the severity of its effects. The ninth Egyptian plague—darkness (Exodus 10:21-23)— was probably in his mind.

8:13. *An Eagle's Triple Cry of Woe.* The seer again effectively uses the device of an interlude. The woeful cry of an eagle in **midheaven** separates the first four trumpet visions, which have involved upheavals of nature, from the final three, which bring direct attacks on human beings. The first woe announced by the eagle is identified in 9:12 with the result of the fifth trumpet blast. The second is identified in 11:14 with that of the sixth. The third is probably the whole series of plagues of the seven bowls narrated in chapter 16.

9:1-12. *A Horde of Demonic Locusts.* With the blast of the fifth trumpet John describes the fall of a **star** from the sky to

earth. The star is personified and represents an angel. **Fallen** means not that the angel is a wicked one, cast out of heaven, but merely "descended." The angel is an agent of God sent to carry out the divine will. He is **given the key to the shaft of the bottomless pit**. Later we are told that he retains that key (20:1).

Bottomless pit translates a single Greek word that has been anglicized as "abyss." It is not to be confused with Hades (Sheol), which is the temporary residence of human souls after death (see above on 1:17-18). Rather this abyss is a place of punishment which burns with **smoke like the smoke of a great furnace**. Thus it resembles the "hell"—literally "Gehenna"—of the gospels and the horrible waterless, fiery chaos described in I Enoch 18:12-16; 19:1-2; 21:1-6. John distinguishes two such places:

  (1) the bottomless pit—the temporary prison of the fallen angels, the demons, the beast, the false prophet, and especially Satan, who is confined there for a thousand years (11:7; 17:8; 20:1-3);
  (2) "perdition" (17:8, 11) or the "lake of fire and sulphur"— the final and unending place of punishment of all these and also of those whose names are not written in the book of life (19:20; 20:10, 14-15).

See further below on verses 11-12.

9:3-6. Out of the smoke of the bottomless pit comes a swarm of **locusts** with **power** to torment **mankind**. Locusts are the eighth of the Egyptian plagues (Exodus 10:4-15), but these locusts are demonic rather than earthly (cf. Joel 1–2). They do no damage with their mouths, as do ordinary locusts. In fact they are expressly forbidden to touch **any green growth**. They have **stings** like a **scorpion**, and it is with these that they inflict **torture**, but a torture short of death. From this demonic torment the 144,000 who have the **seal of God upon their foreheads** (cf. 7:4-8) are protected.

The limitation of the torture to **five months** was no doubt suggested by the fact that the natural locust is born in the spring and dies in the early autumn—thus living for a period of about five months. Verse 6 is a vivid description of the agony suffered by all exposed to the torture.

9:7-10. The seer expands his description of the locusts, drawing in part on material in Joel 1–2. They appear like war **horses. Crowns of gold** mark them as a conquering horde. Their antennae give the appearance of **hair**, and their **teeth** are like those of a lion, their thoraxes suggest **iron breastplates**. The loud rushing **noise** made by their **wings** is like that of **many chariots . . . rushing into battle**—a comparison adopted directly from Joel 2:5.

9:11-12. The locusts' **king** is the ruler of the **bottomless pit** and the demonic powers incarcerated in it. The **Hebrew** name **Abaddon**—literally "destruction"—appears in the Old Testament as a poetic designation of Sheol, the subterranean abode of the dead. **Apollyon**—literally "destroyer"—is the **Greek** equivalent. One of the symbols of the Greek god Apollo was the locust, and plagues and destruction were sometimes attributed to him. Those who see back of John's thought a symbolism derived ultimately from Persian Zoroastrian religion have identified Abaddon-Apollyon here with Ahriman (see below on 12:1-6). After being cast out of heaven he dwelt in the abyss as lord of all evil spirits, hurtful beasts, scorpions, and snakes. On verse 12 see above on 8:13.

9:13-21. *Demonic Horses.* The blast of the sixth trumpet results in the release of a horde of demonic horses—a scene that appears to be a variant of the plague of the fifth trumpet. The author uses familiar Old Testament imagery of the onslaught in the last days of a fierce host of **cavalry**. But he transforms the horses into fiendish monsters, as he has already done with the locusts, and represents them as the instruments of God's wrath on the enemies of the people.

9:14b-15. The **Euphrates** was the easternmost limit of the Roman Empire. During the imperial era there were constant fears of an invasion by the dreaded Parthian cavalry across that river boundary. But the thought of a Parthian invasion is not uppermost in John's mind. The invasion is demonic, not natural. It is the monstrous horses that are the threat, not the horsemen.

The **four angels . . . bound at the great river** are presumably other than the four who stand at the four corners of the earth and hold back the four devastating winds (7:1-3). John can vary and multiply comparable symbols. Though they play no part in what follows, the angels are evidently thought of as the leaders of the invading host of demonic horses. They are **held ready for the hour** when they should slay a **third of mankind**. It was a familiar doctrine in apocalyptic that God had fixed the precise time for every event, and John took over that determinism.

9:16-19. The vast number of 200,000,000 demonic horses is in accordance with John's use of hyperbole and the superlative. The brilliant armor of the **riders** is mentioned, but the stress is all on the fiendish horses. They have **heads . . like lions' heads** (cf. the locusts with **teeth like lions' teeth** of the preceding vision). They belch **fire and smoke and sulphur . . . from their mouths** and do harm also with their **tails**, which look **like serpents, with heads**. Probably the seer's own imagination is responsible for this imagery. Some, however, have pointed to the representation on Greek vases and coins of the chimera, a fire-spouting monster whose fore part was a lion and whose hinder part was a serpent.

9:20-21. Despite the plagues' devastation of a third of all people outside the church, **the rest . . . did not repent**. Though punishment is John's main concern, he holds also that the plagues could have given cause for repentance (cf. Joel 2:12-14). Those who might have done so, however, do not desist from the **immorality** of every description. This, John holds, is the inevitable consequence of the worship of **demons and idols**. His ridicule of idolatry is based on Daniel 5:23.

10:1-11. *The Angel and the Little Scroll.* The first six trumpet visions following one another in rapid succession have ended. Before the seventh—as before the opening of the seventh seal (chapter 7)—the author introduces another dramatic interlude to serve as a preparation and a prelude. The seer has evidently changed his station from heaven (4:1) to earth, though he makes no reference to his shift of place. A **mighty angel**—possibly

Gabriel—descends **from heaven** and the seer is addressed by a **voice from heaven**.

Much of John's vision is dependent on scenes from the opening chapters of Ezekiel. The angel comes **wrapped in a cloud** (cf. Ezekiel 1:4), with a **rainbow** and **fire** (cf. Ezekiel 1:26-28). He holds a **little scroll open in his hand** (cf. Ezekiel 2:9-10). A **voice . . . from heaven** orders the seer to **take the scroll**. The angel bids him **eat** it, warning that it will be **sweet as honey** in his **mouth** but **bitter** to his **stomach** (cf. Ezekiel 3:2-3). After eating the scroll the seer is told to **prophesy about many peoples and nations and tongues and kings** (cf. Ezekiel 3:1).

Other elements in John's vision are drawn from Daniel. The angel has **legs like pillars of fire** (cf. Daniel 10:6). The angel raises his **right hand** and swears **by him who lives for ever and ever . . . that there should be no more delay** (cf. Daniel 12:6-7). The seer is commanded to **seal up** what he has heard (cf. Daniel 12:4, 9).

The **seven thunders** (cf. 8:5; 11:19; 16:18) may recall the sevenfold description of the voice of Yahweh in Psalm 29:3-9 as sounding like thunder and shaking both sea and land.

Virtually all the material in this scene, therefore, is borrowed from Old Testament sources. John interweaves and adapts it to his own dramatic and artistic purpose. The angel bestrides **sea** and **land** and cries with a **loud voice** because his message is addressed to the whole world. The words which John hears but is forbidden to **write** are a foreboding of judgments about to break with the blowing of the seventh trumpet. Then the **mystery of God**—God's whole purpose with respect to the world—will finally be accomplished. John's finding the little scroll sweet in his mouth but bitter in his stomach means that the initial reception of the revelation brings joy but the later realization of its awful consequences brings grief and dismay.

11:1-14. *The Two Heavenly Witnesses.* It is widely held that in this second interlude John has adapted earlier Jewish apocalyptic material to his use. This reworking of an older source would be responsible for much of the difficulty in understanding its message. The reference to the temple in

Jerusalem (verses 1-2) indicates that the source was composed before the destruction of the city and the burning of the temple in A.D. 70.

11:1-2. The seer is commanded to **measure the temple of God**. This opening scene is modeled on Ezekiel 40–43, though there the measurement was preparatory to rebuilding the temple. Here its purpose is to protect those who worship in the temple. Probably the seer thinks of the incident as comparable to the sealing of the 144,000 (chapter 7). The church is to be guarded against the onslaught of demonic powers. The outer court—the Court of the Gentiles, to which non-Jews were admitted—and the **holy city** will be devastated **for forty-two months**. This is the conventional period of three and a half years that in Daniel and in this apocalypse limits the duration of the power of evil. As the Roman army under Titus trampled Jerusalem, so Satan through the agency of the Roman Empire holds sway over the Christians' world.

11:3-4. The seer speaks of the prophecy of the **two witnesses**. God will give them **power to prophesy** throughout that calamitous period—1,260 days equal three and a half years. They are first described with imagery adapted from Zechariah 4:1-14. There **two olive trees** apparently represent Zerubbabel and Joshua. They symbolize the channels through which God's power becomes effective, and they pour their oil into a single lampstand located between them. In John's use of the images both the olive trees and the **two lampstands** symbolize the witnesses.

11:5-6. John does not identify the witnesses by name, but this description of their activities makes clear to whom he is referring. Elijah is said to have called down **fire** on the messengers of King Ahaziah (II Kings 1:9-16). Moses brought a plague of hail mixed with fire on the Egyptians (Exodus 9:23). The **power to shut the sky** and prevent rainfall was given to Elijah (I Kings 17:1). According to the Old Testament the drought during Ahab's reign lasted for less than three years (I Kings 18:1). In the form of the tradition reflected here (cf. Luke 4:25; James 5:17) the period was extended to three and a half years to conform to the conventional symbol for the duration of calamity.

The **power over the waters to turn them into blood** was granted to Moses for the first plague afflicting the Egyptians (Exodus 7:20). Elijah ascended to heaven (II Kings 2:11). According to Jewish tradition Moses too was taken up from the earth by physical levitation. Malachi 4:5-6 predicts the return of Elijah before the expected day of Yahweh. This became the ground for a widely held belief that he would return as a forerunner of the Messiah (cf. Mark 6:15). Deuteronomy 18:15 predicts that God would raise up a prophet like Moses. In some quarters this led to the belief that Moses also would return before the Messiah's advent. In the account of the transfiguration (Matthew 17:1-8; Mark 9:2-8; Luke 9:28-36) the inner circle of disciples sees Moses and Elijah standing with Christ on the holy mount.

11:7-10. The two witnesses are secure from all attacks by enemies while they perform their mission. Then they fall as martyrs when the **beast that ascends from the bottomless pit** overcomes and kills them. The relation of this beast to the two beasts of chapter 13 is unclear. Perhaps it is meant to be the same as the second beast, which rises from the earth (13:11-17). Obviously it shares their character as Antichrist, the enemy of God, Christ, and the Christians.

The **dead bodies** of the prophets are left unburied for the symbolic period of **three days and a half** while non-Christians rejoice. Most interpreters conclude that the **great city which is allegorically called Sodom and Egypt** means Jerusalem. However, some recent writers maintain that it means neither Jerusalem nor Rome but the great city of this world order in contrast to the coming heavenly and eternal order. It is in this world city that Jesus was crucified, Christians are persecuted, and Moses and Elijah in their reincarnation will be killed by the Antichrist.

11:11-14. The witnesses have now become martyrs. They are restored to **life** and reascend **to heaven** in response to a heavenly voice that bids them **"Come up hither!" A great earthquake**

174

destroys a **tenth of the city**, and the **rest** of its inhabitants are filled with fear. They acknowledge the might of the **God of heaven**—without, however, changing their ways. On verse 14 see above on 8:13.

John did not expect that the pagan world will be converted. Its only fate is destruction. The passage as a whole is intended to encourage readers with the thought that their martyrdom, like that of the witnesses, will be followed by God's vindication. Elijah and Moses in their reincarnation, like Jesus himself (cf. 1:5), are prototypes of the victorious martyr. This is probably the right interpretation of one of the most difficult passages in the entire book. The more common interpretation sees it as an assurance that the majority of the Jews in the last days will be converted to Christianity. Under any interpretation the material bristles with unresolved problems.

11:15-19. *Voices and Visions in Heaven.* The blast of the seventh trumpet has been delayed by the interludes described in 10:1–11:14. The blast is followed by an outburst of joy in heaven and responses to it in heaven and in the world of nature. There are similarities between this scene and those described in 4:8-11 and 7:10-12. Here no particular class of the heavenly court is named as those who sing the hymn of praise. It proclaims that the **kingdom of the world**—that is, the rule of Satan—has ended and given place to the eternal **kingdom of our Lord and of his Christ**. It declares that God's sovereign rule over the world is to be completely established.

11:17-18. The anthem of praise with which the **twenty-four elders** respond is an expansion of the preceding hymn. God has now taken the power that God permitted Satan to exercise. The time has come to judge the **dead**, to reward the **saints**, and to destroy the **destroyers of the earth**—namely Rome, Satan, Antichrist, and the false prophet, whose destruction is portrayed in the chapters that follow.

11:19. When God's heavenly sanctuary is opened, John views the **ark of his covenant**. This disappeared at the destruction of the first temple, and Jewish tradition held that it would reappear at the Messiah's coming. Terrible natural phenomena suggest the awful events still to happen.

D. THE DRAGON AND THE LAMB: WARFARE AND VICTORY (12:1–14:20)

12:1-6. *The Heavenly Mother and Her Child.* Various myths of the ancient world told of the escape of a divine child from a superhuman enemy at birth. In this passage the author draws on some version of them. According to a Greek myth the goddess Leto, with child by Zeus, was pursued by the dragon Python. She was brought by Boreas to the sea and handed over to Poseidon, who gave her a place of refuge on an island. There she was safely delivered of the god Apollo. According to Persian mythology Ormazd, the supreme spirit of good, fought with Ahriman (see above on 9:11-12), the supreme power of evil, for possession of the "great royal Glory." Ahriman sent a dragon with three heads to capture it, but it fled to a lake and found refuge with a water spirit. Thus it foiled the dragon's purpose. According to Egyptian mythology Isis, the mother of the gods, was persecuted by a dragon. She fled to an island, where she reared her child Horus. Horus later slew the dragon by his magic arts.

From some such source, no longer identifiable, John has taken this account of a **male child** born of a **sun** goddess, persecuted by a seven-headed **dragon**, and miraculously taken up to the **throne** of God. The purpose of the narrative, of course, is to declare that all the devices of Satan to destroy the Christian Lord were foiled. No parallels between the gospel accounts of the birth of Jesus and this myth are to be noted or looked for. The myth is related as a **portent**, or sign, for the encouragement of Christians under persecution.

12:1-4a. The **woman** is not Mary but a sun goddess. The **moon** is **under her feet** and the twelve constellations of the zodiac are her **crown**, symbolizing her power over human destinies. The seven-headed **great red dragon** is the devil, or Satan (cf. verse

9). The **ten horns** are a symbol of Satan's power as prince of this
world, and the detail is taken from a description of the
one-headed beast of Daniel 7:7. The casting down of a **third of
the stars of heaven** may be a reference to the fall of angels who
are to assist Satan in his evil purposes.

12:4b-6. Satan wishes to destroy the child that is about to be
born lest it should later destroy him, as Apollo destroyed Python
and Horus destroyed the dragon of Egyptian mythology. But
the Messiah is **caught up to God and to his throne**. In language
adapted from Psalm 2:6 the Messiah is described as one destined
to **rule all the nations with a rod of iron**. In verse 17 the woman
is described as the church, the heavenly mother of all
Christians. She is protected and **nourished** in a **place prepared**
for her for 1,260 days, the three and a half years that are
symbolic of the period of calamity.

12:7-12. *Michael's Victory over the Dragon.* The preceding
passage has described an incident **in heaven**, not on earth. The
present one gives a version of the conflict by which Satan was
expelled from heaven. In Daniel 10:21 the archangel **Michael** is
called the patron, or "prince," of Israel. In Daniel 12:1 he is
Israel's defender in the troubles of the last days. Both Michael
and the **dragon** have their **angels**, for the name "angels" can
apply to both good and evil supernatural beings. The war
between the representatives of good and evil is not described.
Only its consequences are noted. Satan and his angels are not
destroyed but **thrown down to the earth**—supporting the
apocalyptic belief that this age is under Satan's control and is
irretrievably evil and corrupt.

12:10-12. The expulsion of Satan assures his ultimate
overthrow. It calls forth an outburst of praise that celebrates the
future triumph as already present (cf. 7:14-17; 11:17-18). The
singers are not identified. If they are angels, they describe
faithful Christians on earth as **our brethren**. If they are martyrs,
they refer in these words to their fellow servants of God on
earth. The defeat of Satan is an assurance that the **kingdom of
our God and . . . of his Christ** is at hand. This will be brought
about by Christ's death and also by the faithfulness of the

martyrs in preferring **death** to the disloyalty of worshiping the emperor. But the hymn has also an anticipation of foreboding. It bewails Satan's increased rage in the persecution of the faithful. **His time is short** both accounts for that rage and encourages those who suffer from it.

12:13-17. ***The Dragon's Pursuit of the Woman.*** Since John is using mythological material and adapting it to his purpose, we cannot press his version of it for consistency. In verses 1-6 the woman is **in heaven**. With this shift in scene she is on **earth**. The dragon, now too on earth, resumes his pursuit of her. In several respects this section parallels the earlier one. Some interpreters see in this an indication that John is using two parallel sources. Probably his wish to reiterate is enough to explain the similarities.

12:13-16. Again the woman escapes to the **wilderness** for safety, this time with the aid of **two wings of the great eagle**. In this place of safety she is again **nourished** for the three and a half years that are the conventional symbol of the time of calamity. Since the woman symbolizes the church, the true Israel, John may have in mind God's words to the Israelites in the desert: "I bore you on eagles' wings and brought you to myself" (Exodus 19:4).

The dragon, now also called the **serpent**, tries to destroy the woman with a flood of **water** spewed from its **mouth**. Some interpreters see here a reflection of an Egyptian myth in which a personification of the Nile attempts to engulf the goddess Isis with a flood (see above on verses 1-6). She is saved by the earth, which swallows the water. Whatever its origin, the scene symbolizes the protection of the church, providentially saved from Satan.

12:17. Foiled in his attempt on the church, the dragon now turns to the **rest of her offspring**. These are identified as the whole body of faithful Christians, those who hold fast to God's **commandments** and **bear testimony to Jesus**. The reading **And he stood** is found in the earliest papyrus manuscript (third century) and in what are usually regarded as the best of the parchment texts. On the strength of this reading it is the dragon who stands on the shore, there to summon the beast from the sea. Some editors prefer the reading "And I stood," referring to the seer, which they believe makes for a better connection with 13:1. Probably it was to make this easier transition that the reading was originally introduced into some Greek texts.

13:1-10. *The Beast from the Sea.* The beast of this passage clearly symbolizes the Roman Empire. The description of it is similar to that of the dragon in 12:3, but here the **diadems** are on the horns. In Daniel 7:6 the four heads of the beast representing Persia symbolize Persian kings. Here the **seven heads** represent Roman emperors, as is explicitly stated in 17:10. The **blasphemous name** must refer to some divine title assumed by the emperors—possibly *divus*, "divine," or Augustus, literally "reverend." The description in verses 1-2 combines into one beast features of the four beasts of Daniel 7—the lion, the bear, the leopard, and the monster with ten horns. It is implied that the beast rises from the sea at the summons of the dragon—that is, Satan—who delegates **his power and . . . throne and . . . authority** to it. The hated Roman Empire is Satanic in origin.

13:3. The head that bears the marks of a **mortal wound** but has been **healed** probably reflects the myth that Nero did not actually commit suicide in 68. It was said that he took refuge in the East and would return leading Parthian kings for the destruction of Rome. At some point in early Christian tradition this expectation that Nero would return was combined with the idea that the Antichrist would rise up with demonic powers to persecute the church. The non-Christian **world** is filled with **wonder** at this marvelous revivification of Nero.

13:4. This is a direct reference to the cult of emperor worship. Worship of the emperor was based on the claim that he was divine. John holds that this worship is actually directed to Satan, who has invested the **beast** with his **authority**. The non-Christian world, awed by the power of the empire, is persuaded that it is invulnerable. The Christian community, however, would be assured that this embodiment of demonic might is shortly to be overthrown by Christ.

13:5-10. The author of Daniel spoke of Antiochus Epiphanes as the incarnation of evil in his time (Daniel 7:25). John speaks of the Roman incarnation of Satanic power. The beast will speak **haughty and blasphemous words** against God and **those who dwell in heaven**. He will prevail for three and a half years, the period predicted in Daniel for Antiochus' supremacy. From the point of view of a resident of the Mediterranean world the Roman Empire could be thought of as embracing the whole earth—**every tribe and people and tongue and nation**. Since emperor worship was enforced on all but Jews, it could be said that **all who dwell on earth** would worship the Roman ruler. The only exceptions to Satan's rule through the emperor cult are the faithful Christians. Their names have been entered before the beginning of time in the heavenly register, the Lamb's **book of life**.

As in the letters to the seven churches (chapters 2–3) the significance of what has been said is to be impressed on all readers. The fatalistic refrain that follows is almost a paraphrase of Jeremiah 15:2. The passage ends with a summons to **endurance** and **faith**, the virtues that mark and support the martyr.

13:11-17. *The Beast from the Land.* A second beast appears, this one from the **earth**. According to ancient tradition there were two monsters—Leviathan dwelling in the sea and Behemoth on the dry land. John may think of the beast from the land as the one already mentioned in 11:7, the beast who ascended from the bottomless pit to kill the two heavenly witnesses. He is called the false prophet in 16:13; 19:20; and 20:10. He gives the appearance of the Christ but reveals himself to the discerning as Satanic, for his voice is like that of a **dragon**.

13:12. This second beast represents the priesthood of the imperial cult. The priests use their **authority** to enforce the worship of the emperor, **the first beast, whose mortal wound was healed**. Verse 3 spoke of the fatal wound of one of the heads of the beast, but here the reference is widened to apply to the beast itself. Thus he is identified with Nero come back to life.

13:13-17. According to Mark 13:22 and II Thessalonians 2:9 **great signs** were expected of the Antichrist. The special miracle in verse 13 recalls that of Elijah (I Kings 18:38). The priests of the imperial cult command the non-Christian world to **make an image for the beast** and establish the fearful alternative of worship or death. To escape death all are required to bear a **mark** showing that they have worshiped the beast. Economic sanctions are imposed as a further lever of enforcement on all who do not exhibit the mark. During Trajan's reign, early in the second century, Pliny's correspondence shows that those who refused to worship the emperor were put to death. It may be assumed that such punishment was already in force in Domitian's reign.

13:18. *The Number of the Beast.* John now makes a cryptic identification of the first beast. His reference is clear, he says, to those who possess the requisite **wisdom.** To interpreters who are no longer within John's frame of reference the meaning is not so clear. In fact any resolution of the enigma remains at best a controlled guess. Some think the explanation is that the thrice-repeated **six** is meant to symbolize evil, since six, falling just short of seven, the perfect number, might carry the sense of imperfection.

More usually the number is regarded as an example of gematria. This was the practice of giving letters of a word or name their numerical equivalent—possible in either Hebrew or Greek, since both used the letters of their alphabets as numbers. The most attractive of the many solutions put forward is that the name is the Greek form Neron Caesar, which when transliterated in Hebrew characters adds up to 666. If the Latin spelling Nero is used, the sum in Hebrew transliteration is 616, which might account for the variant in some Greek manuscripts (see the Revised Standard Version footnote).

14:1-5. *The Bliss of the Redeemed in Heaven.* This scene, with its description of Christ and his followers, stands in dramatic contrast to the preceding. The **Lamb** is set over against the beast. Christ's faithful with his name and that of his Father **on their foreheads** stand over against those who bear the beast's mark. The vision anticipates the end, when the faithful will receive their reward. The 144,000 are probably those already spoken of in 7:1-8 rather than a select class of God's people. **Mount Zion** was traditionally the site where God or the Messiah would summon the faithful Israelites. In this scene John probably thinks of it as located in heaven. However, some interpreters believe the seer is envisaging the time when Christ will establish his millennial kingdom on earth.

14:2-5. **A voice from heaven** is heard, sounding like **many waters** and **loud thunder** and **harpers playing on their harps** (see above on 5:7-8). The singers of the **new song** are not identified. Probably John has in mind an angelic chorus rather than the redeemed, for he says that only they can **learn** the song. In verse 4a the redeemed are described as celibates. Taken literally this might distinguish them from the group of 7:1-8, but the meaning may be figurative. They may represent martyrs who have not yielded to idolatry. They **follow the Lamb wherever he goes**. They are described as **first fruits** because, like the first fruits of the harvest, they are wholly consecrated to God. Their virtues of truthfulness and chastity are emphasized.

14:6-20. *The Doom of Worshipers of the Beast.* The first of several angels announces that God's eternal purpose is about to be fulfilled. **Judgment** is at hand, and God the Creator alone should be worshiped. A **second** angel follows, pronouncing doom over Rome: **Fallen, fallen is Babylon the great** (cf. Isaiah 21:9). The rest of verse 8 is based on the condemnation of Babylon in Jeremiah 51:7. **Her impure passion** refers to her idolatry.

14:9-11. In view of the coming judgment, a **third** angel warns of the terrible punishment that must fall on those who worship the beast. They will **drink the wine of God's wrath**, wine that is undiluted. Isaiah 34:8-10, describing the punishment of Edom, may have been in John's mind when he wrote that the worshipers of the beast will be **tormented with fire and brimstone . . . and the smoke of their torment goes up for ever and ever**.

14:12-13. Verse 12 repeats most of 13:10c, with the additional description of the **saints** as those who **keep the commandments of God and the faith of Jesus**. The steadfastness to which the saints are summoned must involve martyrdom for many of them. With this in view the vision now brings assurance. Those who perish because of their loyalty to their faith during the interval before the final judgment are the objects of God's love and grace. The beatitude is declared by a **voice from heaven** and then echoed by the **Spirit**—the same Spirit who has warned and exhorted the readers of the seven letters (chapters 2–3). Their martyrdom will bring an end of trials and sufferings—no doubt **labors** refers to their activities as Christian witnesses. Their obedience and faith will be remembered at the last judgment. Here, as in 2:23; 20:12-13; and 22:12, John stresses the importance of Christian "works" as a manifestation of loyalty and devotion.

14:14-16. The seer now returns to the impending doom of the worshipers of the beast. As in 1:13, the heavenly Christ at his second coming is described as **one like a son of man**—the phrase borrowed from Daniel 7:13. The **golden crown** symbolizes his regal authority. The **sharp sickle** fits the metaphor of the harvest that follows. Elsewhere the instrument of his wrath is an iron rod or a sharp sword that projects from his mouth. In verses 6-9 three angels have proclaimed the imminence of the judgment. Now **another angel** issues an order to the heavenly Christ that the judgment should be executed. As in 6:9, heaven, God's dwelling place, is portrayed as a **temple**. The angel is thought of as God's messenger to the Messiah, and the command is not the angel's but God's. It is God alone who sets the time of judgment (cf. Matthew 24:36). The reaping of the harvest both here and in verses 17-20 appears to be based on Joel 3:13.

14:17-20. Some interpreters hold that the harvest of verses 15-16 is general—that it portrays the whole judgment as it affects both the righteous and the wicked. Thus Christ can be represented as God's emissary. On the other hand, this vintage harvest pictures God's vengeance on the wicked, and an **angel** with a **sharp sickle** is made the divine agent of wrath. It is not clear that John intended such a distinction. More probably both are parallel representations of the same event, and in both the wicked are the objects of the judgment. If so, an angel fulfills the function here that was ascribed in verses 15-16 to the heavenly Christ. **Another angel** conveys God's command to begin gathering the **vintage of the earth**.

The angel who issues the order is described as one who **came out from the altar**—possibly the same angel who in 8:3 mingles the prayers of the saints with the incense on the golden altar before God's throne. That he has **power over fire** is perhaps an allusion to 8:5, where he is said to have filled the censer with fire from the altar and flung it on the earth. The symbolism of God's judgment on the wicked as the treading of grapes in a **wine press** is probably derived from Isaiah 63:1-6. No doubt **outside the city** means "outside Jerusalem." Apocalyptic writers often placed the final overthrow of God's enemies near Jerusalem. The lifeblood flowing from the wine press will make a river about two hundred miles long (the Greek stadion equaled two hundred yards). If John intended symbolism by his use of 1,600, it is obscure.

E. The Seven Bowls (15:1–16:21)

15:1. *The Last Series of Plagues.* This verse introduces still another sign or **portent**—**seven angels with seven plagues**. These are the **seven bowls of the wrath of God** (16:1) that are to be poured on those who bear the mark of the beast. Probably John thinks of this series as the "third woe" announced in 11:14. It resembles the plagues of the seven seals (6:1–8:1) and the seven trumpets (8:2–11:19). Like the two earlier series of calamities, it is a manifestation of the **wrath of God** on God's enemies. This is the third and last series of seven, but the final destruction of Rome (chapter 17) and the final judgment on the beast and the dragon (19:11–20:10) are still to follow. The **seven angels** no doubt are the traditional seven archangels of late Jewish angelology (see above on 8:2-6).

15:2–16:1. *The Temple in Heaven.* The **sea of glass** has already been mentioned as standing before God's throne in heaven (4:6). Here there is the added detail **mingled with fire**.

The saints who have triumphed over the beast are pictured as standing by the shore of this heavenly sea, holding **harps of God**—that is, for worship (see above on 5:7-8).

15:3-4. The saints sing a hymn of praise to God for his mighty acts, anticipating the final victory and the execution of God's righteous judgments. **Song of Moses** may be an allusion to Exodus 15:1-18, where Moses and Israel sing a song of deliverance after having passed through the sea. Some interpreters think that John has in mind Deuteronomy 32:1-43. It is true that the hymn of the saints has no resemblance to that in Exodus 15, but contacts with that in Deuteronomy 32 are also few and remote. More important is its designation as the **song of the Lamb**, who has delivered the Christian victors. Parallels between several phrases of the hymn and passages in various psalms can be noted:

with **Great and wonderful are thy deeds** cf. Psalms 111:2 and 139:14;

with **Just and true are thy ways** cf. Psalms 145:17 and 119:151;

with verse 4 cf. Psalm 86:9-10; also Jeremiah 10:7.

15:5–16:1. The phrase **temple of the tent of witness** presents difficulties. There is no exact equivalent to the term elsewhere in the Bible, but it would appear to be synonymous with the **temple** of verse 6. The **seven angels with the seven plagues** come from God's dwelling place. They are clothed in **pure bright linen** and like the heavenly Christ (1:13) are **girded with golden girdles**. From **one of the four living creatures** they receive the **seven golden bowls full of the wrath of God**, which are about to be poured out on God's enemies. The **smoke** that fills the temple is a symbol of Gods **glory** and **power** (cf. Isaiah 6:4). God's majesty is so awesome that **no one could enter the temple** until the series of calamities is complete. The **loud voice from the temple** that orders the **seven angels** to inflict the punishments is no doubt the voice of God. The seer has just stated that the temple is unapproachable for the duration of the seven plagues.

16:2. *A Plague of Ulcers.* The first plague is like the sixth

Egyptian plague of boils (cf. Exodus 9:10). The victims of the
foul and evil sores are the men who bore the mark of the beast
and worshiped in its image.

16:3. *The Sea Turned to Blood.* The second plague turns the
sea into coagulated blood, and all marine life is destroyed. Like
the second of the trumpet plagues (8:8-9), this calamity has been
adapted from the first Egyptian plague (Exodus 7:14-25). This
calamity turned the Nile to blood, and all fish in it were
destroyed.

16:4-7. *Fresh Water Turned to Blood.* The third plague turns
all drinking water into blood. This has a parallel in the third
trumpet plague (8:10-11), where a third of the waters become
wormwood and cause "many men" to perish. It corresponds also
to part of the first Egyptian plague, where all the waters of
Egypt, including the water in household utensils, are turned to
blood (Exodus 7:19). There is a guardian **angel of water**—just as
the four winds have their angels (7:1) and fire has its angel
(14:18). In words that echo phrases from the song of 15:3-4 the
water angel praises God's justice in this act of judgment: **It is
their due!** In verse 7 the **altar** is given the power of speech. It
repeats the truth and justice of God's **judgments**. The prayer of
the martyrs in 6:10 for vengeance on the pagan world has been
answered.

16:8-9. *The Sun's Scorching Heat.* The fourth plague causes
the sun to inflict a scorching heat on the wicked. Though they
recognize that God is the source of this and the other plagues,
worshipers of the beast do not **repent**. On the contrary **they
cursed the name of God.**

16:10-11. *Darkness on the Kingdom of the Beast.* The fifth
plague throws the **throne of the beast**, which is Rome, and the
whole Roman Empire into supernatural darkness. No doubt
John has the ninth Egyptian plague in mind—the plague by
which all of Egypt was covered with darkness for a period of
three days (Exodus 10:21-29). Though grievously tortured by
their **pain and sores** the worshipers of the beast persist in their
blasphemy and impenitence. They **cursed the God of heaven
. . . and did not repent of their deeds.**

16:12-16. *The Euphrates River Dried Up.* The sixth plague dries up the Euphrates to allow an invasion of the Roman Empire by Parthian **kings from the east**. The plague has some resemblance to the plague of the sixth trumpet (9:13-21), which releases a horde of demonic horses to cross the Euphrates and slay a third of mankind. Both passages may draw on the widespread belief that a reincarnate Nero would lead the enemies of Rome in a final invasion. The city over which the hated emperor once exercised his tyrannical rule would be devastated.

16:13-14. This vision looks forward to the final battle of the **dragon**, the **beast**, and the **false prophet** with the heavenly Christ (19:11-21). Three demons in the form of **frogs** issue from their mouths. Like the beast out of the earth (13:13-14) they perform **signs** to deceive women and men. They gather the **kings of the whole world**—no longer just the Parthian kings—in preparation for the **battle on the great day of God the Almighty**.

16:15. This warning and beatitude interrupts the flow of the narrative, but it need not be a displacement or an interpolation. It is a dramatic declaration of the suddenness of the end. It gives assurance that those who are ready for Christ's return—who are clothed with **garments** of immortality—are blessed.

16:16. The three demons assemble the forces of the Antichrist **at the place which is called in Hebrew Armageddon**. The site is doubtless the scene of the last great battle between the Antichrist and the Messiah, to be described in 19:11-21. Like the number 666 (13:18) the meaning of Armageddon is obscure. It may be a purely imaginary name for the scene of the final battle. The name does not occur elsewhere in the Bible or in other earlier literature. It is usually interpreted as a compound of the Hebrew word *har*, "mountain," and the name Megiddo. Megiddo was a stronghold guarding the pass across Mt. Carmel into the Plain of Esdraelon, sometimes also known as the Plain of Megiddo. By the "waters of Megiddo" Barak and Deborah defeated Sisera and the Canaanites (Judges 5:19-20). The difficulty with this explanation is that there is no evidence of a mountain named Megiddo. The proposal that the term refers to some mountain in the neighborhood of Megiddo is not wholly satisfactory.

16:17-21. *Storm and Earthquake.* The seventh and last of the bowl plagues affects the **air.** A **loud voice** from the **temple** and the **throne**—the voice of God himself—declares **It is done!** The stage is set for the climactic events of the end. The **voices, peals of thunder, and a great earthquake** have also accompanied the seventh trumpet plague (11:19). The **hail** mentioned in the earlier passage is also brought into this picture. The earthquake of this plague is described as the most disastrous in the history of mankind. Rome—referred to in verse 19 as the **great city** and as **great Babylon**—is **split into three parts**, and the other cities of the empire are utterly destroyed. In this catastrophic manner God vents the full **fury of his wrath.** The predictions of 14:8, 10 are fulfilled. As a further consequence **every island fled away, and no mountains were to be found**—a detail that was part of the disasters following the breaking of the sixth seal (6:14). Though enormous **hailstorms** fall on them **from heaven**, the enemies of God and the church remain impenitent (cf. verses 9 and 11). They respond to the plague only with blasphemy.

F. THE FALL OF BABYLON (17:1–19:10)

17:1-18. *Judgment on Babylon.* One of the **seven angels who had the seven bowls** offers to serve as the seer's guide and interpreter. An interpreting angel is a familiar figure in apocalypses, and in 1:1 John has avowed that his entire series of revelations was communicated to him by an angel. The **great harlot** on whom the judgment is to fall is clearly identified in verse 18 as Rome. The city is described as a harlot because it has seduced people with its cult of emperor worship. Babylon was located on a network of canals that distributed the Euphrates through the surrounding country and is described by Jeremiah as "you who dwell by many waters" (Jeremiah 51:13). Since Babylon for this author is Rome, he transfers the description even though it is not accurate.

17:2-6. The rulers and inhabitants of the Roman world have participated in emperor worship and are described as drunk **with the wine** of that **fornication**. As in 1:10; 4:2; and 21:10, John speaks of himself as **in the Spirit**. In a change of imagery he now sees the harlot seated **on a scarlet beast**. In earlier descriptions the adjective "scarlet" has not been applied to the beast, though the dragon in 12:3 is described as "red." The **blasphemous names** which cover the beast refer no doubt to the various titles of divinity assumed by the emperors (cf. 13:1). According to verses 9-12 its **seven heads and ten horns** symbolize the seven hills of Rome and ten kings.

In verse 4 the harlot's garish garments and luxurious ornaments are described. The detail of the **golden cup** which she holds may be derived from Jeremiah 51:7. It is **full of abominations and the impurities of her fornication**—that is, the idolatry of the imperial cult. As the scarlet beast is covered with blasphemous names, so the scarlet woman bears a name **on her forehead**. It is mysterious and calls for interpretation. It is clear that **Babylon the great** means Rome, the city that is the source of the idolatrous worship of Caesar. In the course of propagating this worship Rome has inflicted martyrdom on Christians who have refused to deny their God. Consequently she can be described as **drunk with** their **blood**.

17:7-8. Now the angel offers an explanation of the scarlet **woman** and the scarlet **beast**. He begins with the beast. Verse 8*a* is almost certainly a reference to the expectation that Nero would reappear in a new incarnation. The angel refers to his rule over Rome, his death, his imprisonment in the abyss, his anticipated return, and his ultimate destruction. The verse then refers to the astonishment of the non-Christian world at the reappearance of the feared and hated emperor.

17:9-11. The explanation becomes more detailed and at the same time more enigmatical. Not only are the **seven heads** the seven hills of Rome; they are also **seven kings**. If it were possible to solve the puzzles of verses 10-12 we might be surer of the date of the book. From whom do we reckon the seven kings? If we start from Augustus and omit the three emperors who ruled only a few months during the interim between Nero and Vespasian, the sixth would be Vespasian (69-79). Titus would then be the seventh, and an anticipated eighth emperor (Domitian) would be represented as a reincarnation of Nero.

If this supposition is correct—and it is problematical at best—and if Revelation comes from the reign of Domitian, the only conclusion we can draw is that John has worked material from the reign of Vespasian into his vision without making it entirely consistent. His own special contribution would then be the identification of Domitian with the reincarnate Nero (verse 11).

17:12-14. There is also no certainty that we can identify the **ten kings**—rulers who have not yet assumed regal authority and who are represented by the **ten horns** of the beast. They may refer to governors of the provinces of the empire. More probably John has Parthian rulers in mind. These are anticipated to be associates and allies. They will cede **their power and authority** to the Antichrist in his effort to destroy the heavenly Messiah. But their attempt will be frustrated. It will be the **Lamb** who will emerge victorious, aided by an army of Christian martyrs. The conquering Christ is given the title **Lord of lords and King of kings**, as in 19:16—but there in reverse order. Verse 14 anticipates the final great battle to be described in 19:11-21.

17:15-18. The angel proceeds with the interpretation. John is told that the **waters** on which the **harlot** is **seated** represent the **dwellers on earth** who have paid homage to Rome and who have been described as drunk with the wine of her fornication (verse 2). Before the final battle against the Lamb, the Antichrist and his associates will turn on the harlot and utterly destroy her. Here again the seer thinks of a reincarnate Nero ravaging the city of Rome, aided by his Parthian allies. In verse 17 the angel asserts that in inflicting this destruction Nero and the kings from the East are actually carrying out God's purpose. The chapter concludes with a clear identification of the great harlot of the vision as the city of Rome.

18:1-24. *Dirge over Babylon.* John views **another angel**—

"another" in contrast to that of chapter 17—who descends **from heaven** and lights all the **earth** with **his splendor**. With a **mighty voice** he sings a dirge over the city of Rome as though it had already been destroyed. The song begins with the words already used in 14:8, **Fallen, fallen is Babylon the great!** which echo the taunt of Isaiah 21:9. The language with which the city's desolation is portrayed in verse 2 recalls Jeremiah 50:39. In verse 3 the reasons for Rome's ruin are briefly stated. The city has seduced the peoples of the empire with the worship of the emperor. All the rulers of the world over which she has imposed her sovereignty have participated in the cult. Furthermore her demand for luxuries has enriched the **merchants of the earth**, who thereby shared in her **wantonness**.

18:4-5. Verses 4-8 are represented as the utterance of **another voice from heaven**. No doubt God is thought of as the speaker, since what is said is directed to **my people**. Christians are told to forsake the city of Rome lest they be tainted by **her sins** and become involved in her punishment. The enormity of the city's sins is stressed, as well as the fact that her punishment is to be a divine visitation.

18:6-7b. The law of revenge is again stated. Rome's punishments are to be in retaliation for her treatment of Christians—a repayment that is to be **double for her deeds**. A **draught** that is twice as deadly as that which she has prepared for others is to be made ready for her. Her torment and grief will correspond to her impious pride and luxury. In her confidence and arrogance she cannot foresee the doom that awaits her.

18:7c-8. Verse 7cd appears to be based on Isaiah 47:8-9, which is directed against Babylon. The plagues that are to be visited on Rome will come suddenly, catastrophically, **in a single day**. They will include **pestilence and mourning and famine** and devastation **with fire**. All these judgments are inescapable, for they are the work of the **Lord God**.

18:9-10. Here the **kings of the earth** who have participated in the cult of emperor worship and have shared Rome's luxury utter their dirge over the devastated city. In a single hour God's judgment has been visited on **Babylon** (Rome), that **great** and **mighty city.**

18:11-17a. The **merchants of the earth** are pictured as joining in the lamentation. With Rome's destruction their trade has come to an end. The catalog of merchandise imported by Rome in verses 12-13 is based on the more detailed and elaborate list of the world's trade with Tyre in Ezekiel 27:5-24. Rome's imports include the necessities of life but also feature luxuries of the most varied kind, as well as **slaves.** The couplet in verse 14 is presumably the utterance of the merchants. The luxuries in which Rome delighted are now lost to it forever. The lamentation of the merchants is given in verses 16-17a. Rome's vast and spectacular **wealth** has been destroyed in a single hour.

18:17b-20. Verses 17b-19 constitute the lament of the mariners and all who do business **on the sea.** In a dirge parallel to those of the kings and the merchants, the mariners bewail the sudden destruction of great Rome. John has drawn here from Ezekiel 27:25-34, where seafarers lament the destruction of Tyre. Verse 20 seems to belong to the mariners' lament, but it can hardly be so interpreted. It is probably the seer himself who calls on **heaven** and its company of Christian martyrs to rejoice over the **judgment** that God has executed on the city of Rome.

18:21-24. This is still another dirge. By a symbolic act a **mighty angel** predicts the destruction of Rome and accompanies his prediction with a song. Both the symbolism of a great **stone** hurled **into the sea** and the content of verse 21bc are suggested by Jeremiah 51:63-64. Old Testament phrases are also adapted and built into much of the rest of the song. For example, cf. verse 22ab with Ezekiel 26:13 and verses 22e-23d with Jeremiah 25:10. With all his borrowing, however, John has woven his material into a structure that is poetic in its own right. The song ends with three reasons why Rome has been destroyed (cf. verse 3):

(1) the power of her **merchants;**
(2) the deception she has imposed on **all nations** by her **sorcery**—probably meaning the propagation of the imperial cult;
(3) the martyrdom she has inflicted on Christians.

19:1-10. *Jubilation over Babylon's Fall.* The scene shifts from earth to **heaven**. There a vast heavenly chorus sings a song that celebrates God's justice in destroying Rome and avenging the martyrdom of faithful Christians. The song has some similarities to that of Moses and the Lamb in 15:3-4. But it is especially reminiscent of the hymns in chapter 5—antiphonal responses, the higher and lower orders of heavenly beings, the prostration before God's throne of the twenty-four elders and the four living creatures, and their response to the chorus. **Hallelujah** is a Hebrew doxology that means "Praise Yahweh!" It occurs often in the Psalms. In the New Testament it is found only in this chapter. With verse 1*b* cf. 12:10. With verse 2*a* cf. 16:7. With verse 2*bc* cf. 17:1-6.

19:3-4. Verse 3 is another brief song of praise. Its one line is a virtual quotation from the description of the burning of Tyre in Isaiah 34:10. In verse 4 the **twenty-four elders** and the **four living creatures** are brought again into the author's vision—and for the last time. They were last mentioned in 14:3. They prostrate themselves and worship before God's heavenly **throne** (cf. 4:10; 5:8) and respond to the heavenly chorus with **Amen. Hallelujah!** (cf. 5:14).

19:5. The **voice** that comes **from the throne** can scarcely be the voice of God, for the doxology it speaks refers to **our God** and **his servants**. It is uncertain whether the seer thinks of the singer as one of the living creatures or as the Lamb. **Praise our God** is a translation of the Hebrew "Hallelujah." The song is a combination of Psalms 134:1 and 115:13.

19:6. The fourth song to begin with "Hallelujah" or its translation is now introduced. The vast **multitude** that sings the song is not identified but is presumably a throng of angels. The description of their singing is reminiscent of that applied to the angelic chorus in 14:2. The opening line of the hymn was the inspiration of Handel's "Hallelujah Chorus." It recalls the words of the twenty-four elders in 11:17. Both passages anticipate the celebration of God's victory and of the inauguration of the kingdom.

19:7-8. The new relationship between God and the people is described as a **marriage**. This is an image found occasionally in the Old Testament (for example, Isaiah 54:1-6; Jeremiah 31:32; Ezekiel 16:8). In the New Testament the image is also applied to Christ and his church. The entrance of God into his eternal reign and the marriage of Christ and the church are parallel ways of expressing the same grounds for joy. In verse 8*b* the seer explains that the **fine linen** with which the church is clothed is the **righteous deeds of the saints**.

19:9. The opening words of this verse read literally: "And he said." No doubt the Revised Standard Version translators are correct in regarding this as a reference to the "interpreting angel" of chapter 17. He bids the seer write a blessing on **those who are invited to the marriage supper of the Lamb** and bears testimony to the truth of this blessing. It was a familiar idea in late Jewish literature that the messianic age would be inaugurated with a banquet (cf. 3:20; Matthew 22:1-14; 25:1-13).

9:10. The angel rebukes the seer when he is about to pay him homage. Worship belongs to God alone. Perhaps, as some interpreters hold, this verse and the comparable passage in 22:8-9 are John's protest against a tendency in Asia Minor to worship angels (cf. Colossians 2:18). The meaning of **For the testimony of Jesus is the spirit of prophecy** is obscure. It may refer to the seer's experience of being "in the Spirit" as he is called and fulfills his mission.

G. THE COMING OF CHRIST TO FULFILL GOD'S PURPOSES (19:11–22:5)

19:11-21. *Christ's Triumphant Appearance.* In this great passage the seer comes at last to the event that has frequently been anticipated—especially in the harvest and the vintage (14:14-20), the battle of Armageddon (16:12-16), and the conflict of the beast with the Lamb (17:12-14). It is an account of the last great battle between the Christ and the Antichrist, of the victory of the former and of the overthrow of the latter. Once again John sees **heaven opened** (cf. 4:1; 11:19; 15:5). The heavenly Christ is seen seated on a **white horse**, the color symbolizing his anticipated victory (cf. 6:2). As in 3:14, he is described as **Faithful and True**. John's words about Christ's righteous judgment echo Isaiah's description of the Messiah in Isaiah 11:3-5.

19:12-13. Repeating a phrase already used in 1:14 and 2:18, John describes Christ's **eyes as like a flame of fire**. As **King of kings and Lord of lords** he is crowned with **many diadems**—cf. the dragon with seven diadems (12:3) and the beast with ten (13:1). The **name** unknown to all but the heavenly Christ is obscure (cf. 2:17; 3:12; 14:1). Presumably it is other than the three listed in this paragraph (verses 11, 13, 16). Some interpreters hold that the author has the name Jesus in mind (cf. Philippians 2:10)—though it is difficult to think of this as a "secret" name. The **blood** with which his **robe** is drenched (cf. Isaiah 63:1) probably is that of his enemies slain in battle. When John gives the heavenly Christ the title **The Word of God** he indicates that he is familiar with the concept in the prologue to the Gospel of John. But he shows no understanding of the religious and philosophical background of the "Logos" idea.

19:14-16. The heavenly hosts that follow the heavenly Christ are probably not angels but Christian martyrs (cf. 17:14). Their **white horses** symbolize the victory they are to gain. The description in verse 15 is compiled from earlier statements in 1:16 and 12:5. The picture of Christ's coming victory as the treading of the **wine press** of God's **wrath** is repeated from 14:19-20. The title **King of kings and Lord of lords** has already appeared in reverse order (17:14).

19:17-21. The climactic battle and its outcome are now briefly described. Carrion **birds** are summoned to gorge themselves on the bodies of those to be slain—much as the prophet Ezekiel is bidden to summon the birds and the beasts to feed on the bodies of Gog and those who are to be killed with him (Ezekiel 39:4, 20). The **great supper of God** stands in gruesome contrast to the marriage feast of the Lamb (verse 9). The enemies of Christ and of the martyrs are enumerated as **the beast and the kings of the**

earth with their armies. The beast is the satanic Roman empire (cf. 13:1-8). The **false prophet** is evidently to be identified with the second beast of 13:11-17, symbolizing the priesthood of the imperial cult. These two will be taken prisoners and hurled alive into the place of everlasting punishment, the **lake of fire that burns with sulphur** (see above on 9:1-12). Their followers will be **slain by the sword** issuing from the mouth of the heavenly Christ, and carrion birds will gorge themselves on **their flesh**.

20:1-10. *The Millennial Reign*. It has been evident that God's judgments in this book are frequently carried out by some representative of the angelic host. The unnamed **angel** of this vision holds the **key of the bottomless pit** and carries a **great chain**. Satan, described as the **dragon**, the **ancient serpent**, and the **Devil**, is bound and thrown into the pit. He is confined in this abyss for a **thousand years**. His power to deceive mankind is thus ended—though the warning is added that, at the end of the millennium, he is to be **loosed for a little while**.

20:4-6. With the casting of the two beasts into the fiery lake and the imprisonment of Satan, the power behind them, the stage is now set for the thousand-year reign of Christ. The company of Christian martyrs is raised from the dead to share this reign **with Christ**. The **rest of the dead**—both the righteous and the unrighteous—are not to be raised until after the millennium. Thus the raising of the select group of martyrs can be described as the **first resurrection**. Those who share in it are declared **blessed and holy**. Their millennial rule with Christ is a foretaste of their eternal happiness, for they will not die at the end of that era.

The idea of an interim messianic age is not original with John. Among other Jewish writings it appears in II Esdras 7:26-30, where the Messiah's reign is said to last for four hundred years, and in II Baruch 39–40. In I Corinthians 15:23-28 Paul seems to presuppose something similar. This idea was probably an attempt to combine two basically different conceptions. The prophets thought of a Messiah who would rule over a purified remnant of Israel on earth. The apocalyptists despaired of any such hope. The present age seemed irredeemably evil and must give way in dramatic fashion to the new and eternal age of God's rule. The doctrine of the interim messianic rule preceding the eternal kingdom preserves the prophetic hope within the framework of the apocalyptic conception.

20:7-10. The last great conflict between Satan and Christ and Satan's final commitment to the place of eternal punishment are now related. With the end of the millennial age Satan is released from imprisonment. He gathers a vast army of followers from all parts of the earth for a final assault. **Gog and Magog** are personifications of Satan's hosts based on various references in Ezekiel 38–39. The assault is made on Jerusalem, which is clearly regarded as the encampment of Christ and his martyrs. The destruction of Satan's army is the work of God. The devil is then cast into the **lake of fire and sulphur** (see above on 9:1-12). He will be tortured forever with the **beast** and the **false prophet**, who have preceded him to that place of torment (cf. 19:20). After all the plagues inflicted on the enemies of God and God's people, on Satan, on the Roman Empire, and on the priesthood of the imperial cult, those enemies are finally and eternally eliminated.

20:11-15. *The Last Judgment.* God alone is the judge at the last trial. God sits on a **great white throne**, the emblem of power and purity. All but the martyrs, who have been raised in the first resurrection (cf. chapter 7), all dead, both just and wicked, stand before the Judge. They are judged from the heavenly records that have been kept—the **book of life** for the faithful (cf. 3:5) and other **books** for the wicked and idolatrous. Their recorded works are the basis of their acceptance or rejection. A general resurrection is presupposed in verse 12 but not actually mentioned until verse 13. The bodies of those who have been drowned are given up by the **sea**—its continued existence when all other creation has passed away is an inconsistent note in the account. The bodies of those who have died in other ways are yielded by **Death and Hades** (see above on 1:17-18). All whose names are not inscribed in the **book of life** are committed to the **lake of fire** (cf. 19:20; 20:10; see above on 9:1-12). For them this is described as the **second death**. Such a description, however, seems hardly appropriate when referring to the fate of Death and Hades, who also are cast into the same place of torment.

21:1-8. *The New Heaven and New Earth.* The seer views a new creation. All that God made in the beginning is removed. With the coming of a new heaven and a new earth John adds that the **sea was no more**. This may be a reflection of Jewish awe and dread before the mysteries and dangers of the vast deep. The **new Jerusalem** descends and is described as a **bride** made ready for Christ (cf. 19:7-9). It is to be the eternal dwelling place of the church, the redeemed community. **God himself** will dwell with the people, will comfort and support them. Grief, pain, and death **shall be no more**. All this belonged to the former age and has no place in the new. God will **wipe away every tear from their eyes** (cf. 7:17*c*; Isaiah 25:8).

21:5-7. God repeats the intention to **make all things new**. God affirms the trustworthiness and truth of the divine assurance—probably the affirmation relates also to the whole book. **It is done!** God's words have come to pass. God's purposes have been accomplished. God speaks as **the Alpha and the Omega**, as in 1:8. Now God adds that this title—the first and last letters of the Greek alphabet—means that God is **the beginning and the end** (cf. 22:13).

In 7:17 the martyrs have been assured that the Lamb would "guide them to springs of living water." In verse 6*b* (cf. 22:17*b*) the promise is repeated **to the thirsty**—that is, to those who yearn for communion with God. There is the added assurance that the life-giving **water** will be provided **without payment** (cf. Isaiah 55:1). In verse 7 the promise is stated in still another form. **He who conquers** is a title that the seer has applied to Christian martyrs in the concluding sections of the letters to the seven churches (chapters 2–3). Such a person will be given the status of God's **son**—a relationship that Paul declares is already the possession of the Christian as a result of the work of the Holy Spirit (Romans 8:17; Galatians 4:7).

21:8. The fate of the wicked is contrasted with that of Christian martyrs. Described as apostates, persecutors of the church, and adherents of the cult of emperor worship, these followers of Satan are to suffer everlasting punishment (see above on 20:11-15).

21:9–22:5. *The Heavenly Jerusalem.* With images drawn in large part from Ezekiel, John describes the new Jerusalem. It already exists in its perfection and splendor in heaven and is now ready to descend on the new earth. The seer's guide, though reintroduced, is presumably the same angel who has been his interpreter since 17:1. The vision has been anticipated in verse 2.

21:10-11. Verses 10-17 are based mainly on Ezekiel's vision of the new temple in Ezekiel 40–48. In a state of ecstasy Ezekiel was set on a high mountain that he might see the new temple of the restored community. Likewise John is borne **in the Spirit** to a lofty eminence whence he can view the descent of the heavenly city. The new Jerusalem has the **glory of God,** God's presence manifests itself in an effulgence of marvelous light, comparable in its brightness and clarity to that emitted by a precious **jewel**.

21:12-14. The picture of a walled city **with twelve gates—** three on each of its four sides, each inscribed with the name of one of the **twelve tribes of the sons of Israel**—is taken over directly from Ezekiel 48:31-34. John adds the detail of the **twelve** guardian **angels.** Here, as in 7:1-8, the twelve tribes symbolize the whole company of Christian martyrs, the new Israel which is assured access to the heavenly city. On the twelve **foundations** to the city's wall, each bearing the name of one of the **twelve apostles,** cf. Ephesians 2:19-20; Matthew 16:18; I Peter 2:5.

21:15-17. The heavenly city is described as a vast cube. Each side measures **twelve thousand stadia**—about 1,500 miles. The imagery of measurement, including the detail of the angel with a **measuring rod,** was suggested by the measurement of the temple in Ezekiel 40–42. **A hundred and forty-four cubits** (twelve times twelve, about 216 feet) almost certainly refers to the thickness of the wall. A wall 216 feet high would be out of proportion to a city 1,500 miles high. **A man's measure, that is,**

an angel's probably means that angelic standards of measurement are the same as those employed by humans.

21:18-21. The precious materials of which the city is constructed are now named. The **wall** is made of **jasper**, the **city** of translucent **gold**, the **foundations of the wall** of twelve different precious stones, the **twelve gates** of **twelve pearls**, and the **street** of **gold**. For this description John draws on the description of Aaron's breastplate in Exodus 28:17-21 and 39:10-14. He has perhaps also used the list in Ezekiel 28:13 of the jewels that adorned the dress of the king of Tyre. The identifications of **agate**, **onyx**, and **carnelian** are doubtful.

21:22-27. In earlier passages John has anticipated a **temple** in the heavenly city (cf. 3:12; 7:15). Now, however, he states that the city will have no temple. The presence of **the Lord God the Almighty and the Lamb** will make any other sanctuary unnecessary. He adds that their **glory** will also make all other sources of illumination unnecessary, whether they be **sun or moon** or **lamp**.

The **nations** of the earth will pay God homage, entering by **gates** that are always open. The continued existence of the Gentile nations in the new era of God's rule was presupposed by the author from whom John is borrowing. His use of this source material without adaptation creates an inconsistency. According to 19:21; 20:7-10; and 20:12-15 none but faithful Christians will survive the events of the last days and the final judgment. But John often did not exert himself to remove inconsistencies. With verse 27 cf. 22:14-15. According to verse 8 those who practice **abomination or falsehood** cannot enter the city because they are in the lake of fire. **Only those who are written in the Lamb's book of life** (cf. 3:5; 13:8; 17:8; 20:12, 15) will share in the new age of God's rule.

22:1-2. The river that flowed out of the garden of Eden and Eden's tree of life (Genesis 2:9-10) are no doubt the ultimate source for the **river . . . of life** and the **tree of life** in the new Jerusalem. But the immediate source is Ezekiel 47:1-12, where a river, issuing from under the temple and with fruit trees on both banks, flows to make the waters of the Dead Sea fresh.

John's river of life flows **from the throne of God and of the Lamb**. His tree of life is used collectively, for like Ezekiel's trees it can be described as on **either side of the river**. Also like Ezekiel's trees it bears **fruit each month** and its **leaves** are **for the healing of the nations**. Probably **twelve kinds of fruit** is John's interpretation of Ezekiel's "fresh fruit every month." It means twelve different kinds in succession rather than at the same time. Since Ezekiel speaks of the fruit as "for food," it is probable that John also thinks of it as nourishment for the dwellers in the heavenly city. The reference to the nations appears to repeat the inconsistency of 21:27.

22:3-5. No person or thing will be permitted in the city that would desecrate it. **The throne of God and of the Lamb** will be there. God's **servants** will **worship him** and **see his face**—that is, experience God's immediate presence. They will bear **his name . . . on their foreheads** (cf. 3:12; 14:1). With verse 5 cf. 21:23, 25*b*. The prophecy that the Lord God will illuminate the saints in the new age and that they will **reign** with God and Christ **for ever and ever** marks the climax of the visions and brings them to an end.

IV. EPILOGUE (22:6-21)

22:6-7. The speaker in verse 6 is presumably the interpreting angel of 17:1 and of the preceding section. He repeats the assurance of 21:5*b* that **these words**—that is, the revelation given to John—**are trustworthy and true**. With verse 6*b* cf. 1:1. **God** is the source, an **angel** is the medium, and faithful Christians are the recipients of a revelation that pertains to the immediate future. The speaker in verse 7, who stresses the imminence of his coming, is almost certainly Jesus Christ himself. Perhaps some indication of a change of speaker has been lost in transmission—or possibly John intended for verse 6 to be understood as spoken by Christ also. The beatitude in verse 7*b* reiterates 1:3*b* and is intended to underscore the seer's authority.

22:8-9. The author once more identifies himself as a certain **John**, as in 1:9. Clearly he was well known to the book's first readers. As in 19:10 he is reproved for attempting to worship his angelic guide. Only **God** is to be worshiped.

22:10-11. The angel is still the speaker and bids the seer: **Do not seal up the words of the prophecy.** The revelation applies to the immediate future. The command reverses the words of Daniel 8:26 and 12:4, 9, where Daniel is ordered to keep his book hidden until the distant "time of the end." Verse 11 is reminiscent of Daniel 12:10. While it is hopeless to look for any change in the wicked (cf. 2:21; 9:20; 16:9, 11), the **righteous** can be exhorted to remain steadfast.

22:12-13. Jesus Christ is again the speaker. Once more he stresses the nearness of the end (cf. verse 7*a*) and the certainty of reward and punishment. In verse 13 he applies to himself the titles that God has used to refer to his own person in 21:6. He adds the additional designation **the first and the last**, which he has used of himself in 1:17 (cf. 2:8). In this book God and Christ tend to merge.

22:14-15. This final beatitude pronounces a blessing on the Christian martyrs. They will be allowed to eat of the **tree of life** and will be granted entrance into the **city**. According to some Greek texts we should read "do his commandments" instead of **wash their robes**. With the former cf. 12:17*b* and 14:13*b;* with the latter cf. 3:4 and 7:14. According to 21:8 the wicked have been consigned to the lake of fire. But in verse 15 John appears to forget this, and pictures them as debarred from the city's gates. Once more we should remind ourselves not to demand too great an interest in consistency from an apocalyptic seer.

22:16. Christ is once more the speaker. He rephrases the assurance of verse 6 (cf. 1:1). He identifies himself as the **offspring of David** (cf. 5:5) and the **bright morning star**. This last is anticipated in 2:28, where it refers to the gift to be granted to the martyrs of Thyatira and appears to symbolize immortality.

22:17. The **Spirit**, speaking through the seer, and the church, designated as the **Bride** (cf. 19:7), join in a prayer for the speedy return of Christ. Those who hear the prayer read in Christian assemblies are invited to join in it also. Those who are spiritually thirsty are summoned to partake of the gift of the **water of life** promised them in 21:6.

22:18-19. The speaker is probably the author. His solemn warning against any changes by addition or omission may be modeled on Deuteronomy 4:2 and 12:32.

22:20-21. Christ's assurance of verses 7*a* and 12*a* that he is **coming soon** is repeated, but this time in a quotation from him rather than directly. **Amen**, literally "so be it," is part of the seer's response to Christ's promise of his speedy advent. **Come, Lord Jesus** translates a Greek ejaculation that Paul quotes in its original Aramaic form, Maranatha (I Corinthians 16:22). Verse 21 provides the concluding epistolary benediction that was missing from the seven letters of chapters 2–3 and gives an epistolary form to the whole book.

FOR FURTHER STUDY

THE LETTER TO THE HEBREWS

James Moffatt, *Hebrews*, 1924. T. H. Robinson, *Hebrews*, 1933. William Manson, *Hebrews*, 1951. A. C. Purdy in *Interpreter's Bible*, 1955. Antony Snell, *The New and Living Way*, 1959. Erich Dinkler in *Interpreter's Dictionary of the Bible*, 1962. F. F. Bruce in *Interpreter's Dictionary of the Bible Supplement*, 1976.

THE LETTER OF JAMES

J. H. Ropes, *A Critical and Exegetical Commentary on the Epistle of St. James*, 1916; a scholarly commentary based on the Greek text. Alexander Ross, *Commentary on the Epistles of James and John*, 1954; a conservative commentary, thorough and scholarly. E. C. Blackman, *The Epistle of James*, 1957; a very good popular commentary. Bo Reicke, *The Epistles of James, Peter and Jude*, 1964. B. S. Easton in *Interpreter's Bible*, 1957. A. E. Barnett in *Interpreter's Dictionary of the Bible*, 1962. R. B. Ward in *Interpreter's Dictionary of the Bible Supplement*, 1976.

THE LETTERS OF PETER

E. G. Selwyn, *The First Epistle of St. Peter*, 1946. F. W. Beare, *The First Epistle of Peter*, 1947. A. M. Stibbs, *The First Epistle General of Peter*, 1959. William Barclay, *The Letters of James and Peter*, 2nd ed., 1960. C. E. B. Cranfield, *Peter, I and II, and Jude*, 1960. J. W. C. Wand, *The General Epistles of St. Peter and St. Jude*, 1934. A. M. Hunter, *Interpreting the New Testament, 1900-1950*, 1951.

THE LETTERS OF JOHN

Commentaries: A. E. Brooke, 1912; C. H. Dodd, 1946; A. N. Wilder in *Interpreter's Bible*, 1957; Neil Alexander, 1962. Expositions: Robert Law, *The Tests of Life*, 1909; Charles Gore, *The Epistles of John*, 1920; G. B. Caird in *Interpreter's Dictionary of the Bible*, 1962; D. M. Smith in *Interpreter's Dictionary of the Bible Supplement*, 1976.

THE BOOK OF JUDE

James Moffatt, *The General Epistles*, 1928. J. W. C. Wand, *The General Epistles of St. Peter and St. Jude*, 1934. William Barclay, *The Letters of John and Jude*, 1961.

THE REVELATION TO JOHN

I. T. Beckwith, *The Apocalypse of John*, 1919; for advanced students. R. H. Charles, *Revelation*, 2 volumes, 1920; for advanced students. Martin Kiddle, *Revelation*, 1940. E. F. Scott, *The Book of Revelation*, 2nd edition, 1949. T. S. Kepler, *The Book of Revelation*, 1957. Martin Rist in *Interpreter's Bible*, 1957. T. F. Torrance, *The Apocalypse Today*, 1959. C. M. Laymon, *The Book of Revelation*, 1960. J. W. Bowman in *Interpreter's Dictionary of the Bible*, 1962. E. Shüssler Fiorenza in *Interpreter's Dictionary of the Bible Supplement*, 1976.

ABBREVIATIONS AND EXPLANATIONS

ABBREVIATIONS

D — Deuteronomic; Deuteronomist source

E — Elohist source
Ecclus. — Ecclesiasticus
ed. — edited by, edition, editor
e.g. — *exempli gratia* (for example)
ERV — English Revised Version
esp. — especially

H — Holiness Code

J — Yahwist source
JPSV — Jewish Publication Society Version

L — Lukan source
LXX — Septuagint, the earliest Greek translation of the Old Testament and Apocrypha (250 B.C. and after)

M — Matthean source
Macc. — Maccabees
MS — manuscript

N — north, northern
NEB — New English Bible

P — Priestly source
p. — page
Pet. — Peter
Phil. — Philippian, Philippians
Philem. — Philemon
Prov. — Proverbs
Pss. Sol. — Psalms of Solomon
pt. — part (of a literary work)

Q — "Sayings" source

rev. — revised
RSV — Revised Standard Version

S — south, southern

trans. — translated by, translation, translator

viz. — *videlicet* (namely)
Vulg. — Vulgate, the accepted Latin version, mostly translated A.D. 383-405 by Jerome

W — west, western
Wisd. Sol. — Wisdom of Solomon

QUOTATIONS AND REFERENCES

In the direct commentary words and phrases quoted from the RSV of the passage under discussion are printed in boldface type, without quotation marks, to facilitate linking the comments to the exact points of the biblical text. If a quotation from the passage under discussion is not in boldface type, it is to be recognized as an alternate translation, either that of another version if so designated (see abbreviations of versions above) or the commentator's own rendering. On the other hand, quotations from other parts of the Bible in direct commentary, as well as all biblical quotations in the introductions, are to be understood as from the RSV unless otherwise identified.

A passage of the biblical text is identified by book, chapter number, and verse number or numbers, the chapter and verse numbers being separated by a colon (cf. Genesis 1:1). Clauses within a verse may be designated by the letters *a, b, c,* etc. following the verse number (e.g. Genesis 1:2*b*). In poetic text each line as printed in the RSV—not counting runovers necessitated by narrow columns—is accorded a letter. If the book is not named, the book under discussion is to be understood; similarly the chapter number appearing in the boldface reference at the beginning of the paragraph, or in a preceding centered head, is to be understood if no chapter is specified.

A suggestion to note another part of the biblical text is usually introduced by the abbreviation "cf." and specifies the exact verses. To be distinguished from this is a suggestion to consult a comment in this volume, which is introduced by "see above on," "see below on," or "see comment on," and which identifies the boldface reference at the head of the paragraph where the comment is to be found or, in the absence of a boldface reference, the reference in a preceding centered head. The suggestion "see Introduction" refers to the introduction of the book under discussion unless another book is named.

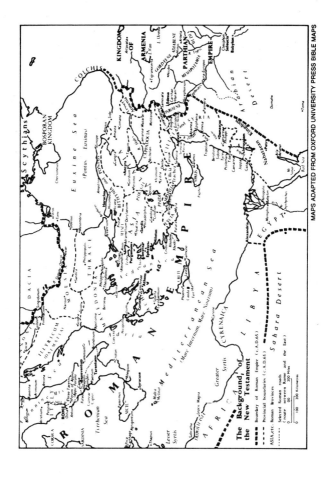

The Background of the New Testament